Domenico Ghirlandaio. AN OLD MAN AND HIS GRANDSON. About 1480. Louvre Museum, Paris

The Story of Painting

H. W. Janson and Dora Jane Janson

The Story of Painting

FROM CAVE PAINTING
TO MODERN TIMES

Harry N. Abrams, Inc., *Publishers*

NEW YORK

On the jacket:
Monet. WILD POPPIES (*portion*). Louvre Museum, Paris

MILTON S. FOX, Editor
Library of Congress Catalog Card Number: 66–18590
All rights reserved. No part of the contents of this book may be
reproduced without the written permission of the publishers
Harry N. Abrams, Incorporated, New York
Printed and bound in Japan

TABLE OF CONTENTS

HOW PAINTING BEGAN

PEOPLE ALL DREAM, WHETHER THEY WANT TO OR NOT. Even animals dream. A cat's ears and tail sometimes twitch in his sleep, while dogs whine and growl and paw the air, just as if they were having a fight. Even when they are awake, animals "see things," so that a cat's fur will rise on his back, for no apparent reason, as he peers into a dark cupboard. And we, too, have goose pimples when we feel frightened.

That is imagination at work. People are not the only animals who have imagination, but we are the only ones who can tell each other about it. If we tell each other in words, we have made a story out of it, and if we take a pencil and draw it, we have made a picture. To imagine means to "make an image" or a picture, in our minds.

There are many different ways for our imaginations to get started. Thus it may happen, at times when we are ill in bed with nothing to do, that a crack in the ceiling will suddenly begin to look like an animal or a tree after we have kept our eye on it for some time. Our imagination fills in the lines that aren't there. Even an ink blot on folded paper (figure 1) will make us think of a lot of other things, although it was made entirely by accident. Psychologists know this and have made up ink-blot tests to find out what is on our minds; for each of us, depending on the sort of person we are, will see different pictures in the same blot.

1. Ink blot on folded paper

WK 1

2. BUFFALO. From an Old Stone Age painting in the Cave of Font-de-Gaume, France

THE MAGIC PICTURES OF THE CAVEMEN

IN THE OLD STONE AGE, SOME 20,000 YEARS AGO, when the first pictures were made, people lived in caves, and their main concern was how to find enough to eat. They had not yet learned how to keep cattle, and they did not know about farming, so they depended mainly on hunting for their food supply. When the hunting had not been good, they had to go hungry. There were, of course, all sorts of birds and fish and small animals they could catch, but these were not enough to live on, so they always hoped to kill something big, like a deer or a buffalo, which would yield enough meat to last them several weeks. They wanted very badly to kill these animals, but they were afraid of them, too, for they only had the simplest of weapons as yet. In fact, since they knew nothing about metal, whatever tools they possessed were made of wood, bone, or stone. And they had to hunt on foot because they had not yet learned how to ride horses.

No wonder, then, that the cavemen's minds were always full of the idea of hunting large animals for food, and of how dangerous this was. And because they thought so much about these things, it is not surprising to find that almost all of their paintings are of these animals, which always look very powerful and lifelike (figures 2 and 3).

How did the cavemen learn to make such skillful pictures? We don't really know for sure. But since the pictures are done on the sides of caves, which are rough and bumpy, it is possible that the idea of making pictures came from these bumps, just as the ink blot suggests ideas to us. Some hungry caveman, staring at the wall of his cave, imagined that a particular bump looked like an animal and perhaps drew an outline around it with a burned stick from

3. WILD BOAR. From an Old Stone Age painting in the Cave of Altamira, Spain

8

4. WILD ANIMALS. From the walls of the Cave of Lascaux, France

the fire. He could then complete the picture by filling in the parts that were not there, and finally he learned how to make such a drawing without the help of the bump on the wall of the cave.

The buffalo and the boar on page 8 are modern copies of cave paintings. Our next picture (figure 4) is a photograph that shows you a cave wall as it really looks, and you will notice that the animals are all scrambled together, without any kind of order. Once you get them sorted out, you can recognize each one easily. Why, then, did the cavemen spoil their pictures by doing one on top of another? It is because they did *not* want them for decorations. Even if the pictures were not such a jumble, we could tell this from the fact that all the caves that have pictures in them are very dark and difficult to get into.

If the cavemen artists had done their animal paintings merely for pleasure, they would have put them near the entrance of the cave, where everybody could look at them. As it is, they are so far back in the caves and so well hidden that they have been discovered only recently, and then by chance. The cave in figure 4 was, in fact, found in 1940 by some boys who had gone out hiking with their dog. Suddenly the dog was gone. They could hear him barking somewhere under the earth, but they could not see him until they found the hole, overgrown with brambles and weeds, through which he had fallen into the cave.

But what were the pictures for, then? They must have been a kind of hunting magic, because some of the animals have spears or arrows sticking into them. The cavemen must have thought that if they made a painting that looked real, and then "killed" it, it was almost like killing the animal itself. Perhaps they threw stones or jabbed the picture with their spears, too. This made them feel stronger and surer, so that when they finally went out to hunt that buffalo, they had a better chance to get him because they were no longer afraid. Once they had "killed" the picture, they did not care about it any more. One cannot kill a real ani-

9

mal twice, and so they felt that one cannot kill a painted animal twice, either. The next time they got ready to hunt, they had to make a new picture to "kill" first.

It is remarkable that the cavemen took so much trouble with their animal paintings. After all, they were going to use them only once. Perhaps they felt that the magic would work best if the animal looked as much like the real thing as possible. And they were probably right, since they used the pictures as targets to practice on, to learn exactly where to hit the animal in order to bring it down.

In any case, it took a good deal of skill to make such convincing pictures. There must have been some cavemen who were better at this than the rest—who had special talent for art. After a while they were probably allowed to stay home and practice making pictures, while all the others had to go out hunting. Even 20,000 years ago, then, the painter was a special kind of person, although we might say that he was mainly supposed to be a magician.

Today we no longer believe in that kind of magic. We know better than to confuse living things with the pictures of these things. But even now our feelings sometimes get confused, no matter what our reason tells us. For instance, it still happens that after a sudden quarrel people will tear up the photograph of someone they used to love; they know quite well that they cannot actually hurt anybody by doing so, yet it gives them great emotional satisfaction. Therefore, it need hardly surprise us that the men of the Old Stone Age, who understood far less than we do about the difference between thinking and feeling, could confuse pictures with real things.

Art is always as much concerned with the way people feel about things as it is with the way things really are. Usually, both knowing and feeling go to make up a picture, and so paintings are different from one another, depending on whether the artist was more interested in what he saw or knew, or in what he felt; also on *how much* he saw, and knew, and felt. ~~Stop~~

PICTURES FOR THE DEAD: EGYPT

THE CAVE PICTURES TELL US A GOOD DEAL about life in the Stone Age, and also about the way our imagination works. We say "our" imagination, because the minds of the cavemen were not really so very different from our own, otherwise we would not understand their pictures as well as we do. The difference between us and the cavemen is not in the kind of minds we have. It is in the things we think about and feel about. Perhaps pictures will also help us to understand how men managed to leave the life of the Stone Age behind and how, over many thousands of years, they gradually changed into the kind of people we are today.

When we speak of these changes we call them *history*. There are many ways of looking at history. Perhaps the simplest is to ask ourselves about the main differences between us and the men of the Stone Age. Even though the cavemen had far greater physical strength than

10

WK 4

5. MEN, BOATS, AND ANIMALS. From a wall painting at Hieraconpolis, Egypt

we do, their life was very much more dangerous than ours—and also much less interesting. The big animals they hunted were really their masters, because the people depended on them so completely. When the animals moved away, they had to move, too, so they never built houses for themselves, only rough shelters. And if they could find no animals to hunt, they starved. In the Stone Age, men worked together only in hunting (and the painters helped, too, with their magic) but today we cooperate in a thousand complicated ways, so that we depend on each other much more than the cavemen did.

Now, this modern way of living could come about only because we are very much more orderly than the people of the Stone Age. We think ahead. We *plan* things, while the lives of the cavemen were just as disorderly as their paintings. How did people discover the need for order? Just as soon as they found out that there were ways of controlling their supply of food instead of letting the food supply control them. First they learned how to tame and keep some of the animals they had hunted before. They became herdsmen who moved about with their sheep, or goats, or cattle, or camels, always looking for grazing lands.

Other people found a different and even better way to control their food supply. They tamed not only animals but plants, too, collecting the seeds and growing their own crops. In order to do this, they needed a warm climate and a good source of water. That is why the first farmers settled along the banks of the big rivers, such as the river Nile, in Egypt. And we shall now take a better look at these old Egyptians, because the history of Europe and America really begins with them. When they started planting their grain, they also planted the seeds of a way of life which has grown into our own way of life today.

The picture on this page shows you a part of the oldest painting in Egypt. It was made on the wall of a temple or tomb in a place called Hieraconpolis, on the banks of the river Nile, almost 6000 years ago. There are some lively animals in it, and people fighting with them and with each other. The big white shapes are boats. At this time, then,

11

the Egyptians still did a lot of hunting, but they no longer depended on it as the cavemen had. They knew how to make and use all sorts of tools, for they built solid buildings of brick and stone, with smooth walls, and boats for sailing up and down the river. There must have been many separate tribes or states along the valley that made war on each other. Notice the two men in the lower right-hand corner: the one with the white, dotted body is beating the one with the black body, who belongs to another tribe.

If you compare this picture with the cave paintings, you will find that the figures in it are not nearly so real looking. There is no shading such as we see in the boar (figure 3). They seem flat, as if they were glued to the wall, and the artist has left out many details. He uses a kind of shorthand, the way modern comic strips sometimes do, so that a circle with a dot in it stands for a face, a crooked line for an arm, and so on.

As a matter of fact, the Hieraconpolis painting was probably meant to tell a story, somewhat like a comic strip. At the time it was made, the Egyptians had just invented the earliest kind of writing, which was done with pictures and is called hieroglyphics. The painter now was also a writer. When he had to tell a story he did it with these simple figures, which were actually "letters" or "signs" that stood for things or words. Because the figures were used over and over again, they became less and less real looking as time went on. We say they became "conventional" or "stylized"—and at last they turned into the letters of our own alphabet, which are no longer pictures at all.

There is something else we notice about the Hieraconpolis painting. We cannot tell whether or not the figures in it are supposed to be connected in some way, because there is no "setting," no indication of landscape or even of the ground they stand on. But there is no messy overlapping, either, and the artist has been careful to spread the figures evenly over the whole surface of the wall. These animals, then, were not made to be "killed" for hunting magic. They were meant to be permanent. But Egyptian painting is connected with another, more complicated kind of magic; and in order to understand that we must know something of Egyptian ideas about religion, and especially about life and death.

When the Egyptians settled down to farming, order and planning became much more important to them than ever before. They had to know when to plant and harvest their crops. So they began to observe the regular movements of the sun, the moon, and the stars, and made up a calendar almost as good as our own. They also kept written records. But the Egyptians found that their harvest depended on a great many things besides the time of year. If the weather was bad, or if they did things the wrong way, they would not have enough food for the winter.

It was hard for them to understand why this sometimes happened, while at other times everything turned out just right. The only explanation they could think of was that the sun, the moon, the clouds, the water, the animals, the plants, and even the earth itself, were all inhabited by powerful spirits that could be either helpful or harmful, depending on

6. HARVEST SCENES. From a wall painting in a tomb at Thebes, Egypt

whether they liked you or not. The more important among these "nature spirits" came to be worshipped as gods. The Egyptians thought of them as great rulers similar to their own kings, except that they were wiser and lived forever.

"Forever" was a very important idea with the Egyptians. They believed that men, too, had a vital spirit, or soul, inside them, and that when a person died his soul would leave his body and keep on living separately. But they also thought that in this "afterlife" the soul still needed a body to come back to. Because of this, they went to great trouble to preserve the bodies of the dead—they made mummies of them by drying them and wrapping them up, and then put them in strong tombs made of stone, so nobody would disturb them. Their kings, the Pharaohs, and other important and wealthy people even had statues of themselves placed in their tombs, as "replacements" if something should happen to the real body.

They also believed that the spirit of the dead needed the same material things as a living person, so they furnished their tombs like a regular household, except that everything

13

was made to last forever. Now, of course, even the richest man could not take all the things he owned with him into the tomb, such as his land, his animals, and his servants. Instead, he had pictures of them made on the walls, where his spirit would find them.

Figure 6 shows you such a wall painting, or "mural," from a tomb in Thebes, done about 2000 years after the one from Hieraconpolis. It was painted almost exactly 1400 years before the birth of Christ, during a period of Egyptian history known as the Empire, when the power of the Pharaohs reached far beyond the Nile valley proper into the neighboring regions to the East and South. At the top of the mural, the dead man's servants are measuring a wheatfield with a rope. At the bottom, they are cutting the wheat with sickles, while the dead man himself sits under a canopy which protects him from the sun. In the center, there are his chariot and some servants measuring a pile of grain. This harvest scene strikes us as very orderly and carefully drawn. The figures no longer look as if they were floating —they have their feet firmly on the ground, even if the ground is only a thin, straight line. We can also tell right away what they are doing.

Still, the picture is not very lifelike. For one thing, the figures are put together in a strange way: their heads, arms, and legs are shown from the side, while the bodies and the eyes are seen from in front. Now, the artist must have known that we don't see people that way in real life. In real life, we never get a very good view of anything in one glance, because most things are round rather than flat, and we can see only one side of them at a time. We don't really mind this, for if we want to know what is around the corner, we just walk up to it and then take another look; or if we see somebody's back and want to know what his face is like, we wait until he turns around. But we can't walk through a picture, and the figures in it cannot turn around. So the Egyptian painter made up for this by inventing a special kind of human figure where all the important parts of the body show up equally well in one view. He also knew that in real life a harvest is a complicated business, with many people doing different things one after the other. We would have to watch them for quite some time if we wanted to understand what they are doing. How could the same story be told in a picture, where there is no space and no movement?

The Egyptian artist realized that a lifelike painting, of the kind the caveman had done, was not what he wanted, because it would let him show the harvest only the way it looked at one particular moment, and not the whole story of the harvest. And since he was working to please the spirit of a dead man, the story had to be complete; otherwise the spirit might miss something. So our painter has made everything much clearer and more orderly than it ever is in real life. His figures are spread out on the wall, and they overlap only when several of them are doing the same thing; some are extra large, to show that they are more important than the others. And if he wants to tell us that something is far way, such as the three trees in the top strip, he puts it above, not behind, the figures in the foreground.

Our painter, then, does not show us what he actually *sees*, but what he *knows*. He fol-

7. WILD BOAR HUNT. Part of a wall painting from the Palace of Tiryns, Greece

lows a strict set of rules, which we call the Egyptian "style"—the Egyptian painter's way of doing things. These rules may strike us as a bit peculiar at first, but after a while we come to feel that they are really very wise and well thought out. Sometimes, too, the rules could be broken. Look at the horse in our picture: its dappled color, its prancing movement make it seem much gayer and livelier than the rest. Now, horses were unknown in Egypt when the rules for painting were set up. They came to the Nile valley only 200 years before the date of our picture, which was not a very long time for the Egyptians, so our painter did not know how to apply his rules as strictly as usual in this case. And that is why the horse looks so much less "frozen" than the other figures. Stop

PICTURES FOR THE LIVING: CRETE

IF YOU TOOK A SHIP from the mouth of the Nile and sailed north and a little to the west on the Mediterranean Sea, you would come to a long, rocky island called Crete, and then to the southern tip of Greece. There, between 2500 and 1000 B.C., you would have found a marvelous nation of sailors quite unlike the Egyptians. While the riches of Egypt came mainly out of the Nile valley, the Cretans were bold traders and pirates who made up for the poor soil of their homeland by bringing in food and many other important things from all the countries round about.

We have recently learned how to read their writing, so that we are beginning to know something about them. But from the ruins of their palaces, some of which have been dug up and partly rebuilt, and from the pictures they did, we can guess that they were just about the richest and happiest of the early Western nations. One of the palaces even had toilets that flushed, something almost unheard of until about a hundred years ago.

8. Upper part of a "geometric" vase from Attica. Eighth century B.C., Metropolitan Museum of Art

The wild boar hunt in figure 7 is a Cretan painting from the walls of the Palace of Tiryns, in southern Greece, done about 1200 B.C. Unfortunately, only a small portion of it has come down to us, so we can no longer see the hunter whose hand, on the right, sticks a spear into the animal. But what is still there—the racing hounds and the ferocious, galloping boar—reminds us more of the cave paintings, with the vigorous, real looking animals, than it does of the "frozen" Egyptian style. Still, the Cretan painter must have learned something from the Egyptians, for his picture, despite its rapid movement, is an orderly scene, not just a wild tangle of animals. And like the Egyptians, too, he makes his forms cling to the wall, and follows definite rules—the three dogs are all done from the same pattern, except for their spots. There is no hunting magic here, but there is no service of the dead, either. For the Cretans, boar hunting was a sport, and the picture was done not from fear but for pleasure. It tells us of the thrill of the chase, and of the enjoyment of nature that we find in all of Cretan art. The gay and graceful shapes, the clear colors, must have made it a splendid decoration for the palace wall.

Stop

GREEK AND ROMAN PAINTING

THE CRETANS WERE CONQUERED, and their palaces destroyed, by warlike tribes that came into Greece from the north around 1100 B.C. These Greek tribes also learned a great deal from the Cretans, and this helped them to build up a great civilization of their own— greater, in some ways, than any the world has seen since. They soon settled and formed separate states, each named after its main city. Athens, in the region we call Attica, became the most important of these city-states, and it was there, between the eighth and the third century B.C., that the Greeks produced their keenest thinkers and their finest artists.

When we talk about the masterpieces of Greek art, we usually think of temples and statues, and not of paintings. That is because quite a few of the famous temples and statues

16

WK 9

are still there, while the paintings that used to be on the walls of the temples and houses have all been destroyed. We can read about these pictures in ancient writings. And we know that the Greeks were just as proud of their great painters as they were of their architects and sculptors. Fortunately, however, we have lots of Greek painted pottery (or "vases," as we call them, although they were made to hold wine or oil or water, rather than flowers). These vase paintings are often very beautiful, but of course they are much simpler than the large pictures were. From them we can get at least an idea of what the lost wall paintings must have been like.

In figure 8 you see the top part of a very early vase, from the eighth century B.C. Most of the forms are made up of triangles and squares, and everything is fitted into such a tight pattern that it takes us a while to realize that this is a scene of mourning: in the middle, the dead man is stretched out on a simple bed, and there are long lines of people on both sides, wringing their hands or tearing their hair in sorrow. How different this is from the Egyptian paintings, where nobody ever betrays his emotions. Here for the first time we find a picture of people not only *doing* things but *feeling* things. This shows us that the Greeks, from the very beginning, were much more interested in the living than in the dead. To them, life was an exciting and glorious adventure, not just a time to prepare for death. The dead, they thought, were only shadows whom nobody had to fear.

Our next vase (figure 9) was made about 500 B.C., in a style called Archaic to distinguish it from the earlier, Geometric style. It is painted in black and dark red against the natural clay color of the vase. The lines inside the figures are made by scratching away the paint with a needle. This illustration shows us the hero Hercules wrestling with a lion. The Greeks believed that Hercules became a god instead of a shadow after he died, because he was so brave and strong. Their gods behaved very much like a family of human beings—they quarreled among themselves, fell in love, or played jokes, and when they liked somebody especially they would adopt him as one of their own. The two figures on our vase are a bit stiff in the joints, because the Archaic artist was still using pretty much the same rules as the Egyptian painters. But they are also full of en-

9. HERCULES AND THE LION. Black-figured vase from Attica. Metropolitan Museum of Art

17

10. BRIDAL SCENE. From a red-figured Attic vase. About 420 B.C., National Museum, Athens

ergy and spirit, and that is exactly what the Egyptian painters had left out of their pictures.

In the hundred years that followed, the Greeks concentrated more than ever before on facing the problems of this world instead of the next. They completely discarded all the age-old painting rules which the Egyptians had so carefully worked out and which had stuck in everybody's mind for thousands of years. Look at figure 11, a pottery disk done about 460 to 450 B.C. in what we call the Classic style. The painter has used several colors on a white ground, almost as if he were working on a piece of paper, and the picture does indeed look much more "modern" than those we have seen before. The lines are no longer scratched in but drawn with a brush, so that they flow more gracefully and smoothly.

But the most remarkable thing about these lines is that they somehow make the figures look round and natural, rather than flat. If you compare the disk with the archaic vase, you will see why: in the Hercules, we still find the old combination of front and side views, but the young man in the picture opposite is drawn the way he would actually look from where we stand, so that we see much more of his left side than of his right. The right shoulder, for instance, is strongly foreshortened—it looks much smaller than the other. But exactly because of this we get the impression that it is farther away from us, and this makes us feel that the entire figure reaches back into space instead of sticking to the surface of the picture.

Figure 10 shows a slightly later example of the Classic style, and is even more freely drawn; the figures have even greater roundness. It comes from a vase which was a wedding present and shows the crowning of the bride—a part of the wedding festivities—and the bringing of presents. Here the artist has sketched his figures directly on the red clay body of the vase, and then filled the spaces in between with black. These graceful young women, stand-

18

11. Goddess Offering a Ribbon to a Youth. Painted disk. 460–450 B.C., Metropolitan Museum of Art

ing or sitting with such ease and assurance, make us feel completely at home. We must not think, however, that they were meant to be portraits. The Classic Greek artist was not yet interested in particular people, with all their personal imperfections; he preferred to make all his figures as beautiful as he could—he idealized them.

Only in later times, when Greek art had spread to all the countries around the Mediterranean Sea, do we find real portraits, such as the very fine one in figure 12. It comes from Egypt, about the third century A.D., but its style and technique are Greek. The picture is done on a wooden panel, and the colors are not mixed with water, as in all the paintings we have seen so far, but with hot wax. This makes a thicker, creamier kind of paint, which allows the artist to model his forms by blending light and dark shades of color right on the panel.

The man who painted our portrait has done a wonderful job of modeling; that is one reason why his work looks so three-dimensionally solid and real. But our painter also had a special feeling for all the little things that serve to make this boy's face different from anybody

19

12. PORTRAIT OF A BOY. From Fayum, Egypt. Metropolitan Museum of Art

else's: the stubby nose, the square jaw, the small, curved mouth and the dark, shiny eyes. Of course the picture has style, too—otherwise we could not tell it from a snapshot—but we find it difficult to say just what this style is, since everything seems so fresh and natural to us. If we did not know that our picture was done more than seventeen hundred years ago, we might well think that it was painted only yesterday.

The technique of painting with wax could be used not only on wooden panels but also on the walls of houses. However, the favored technique for mural painting in ancient times was a method called "fresco," which means that the artist worked with water colors on the freshly applied, moist plaster. The Romans were particularly good at this, as we know from the many murals that have been dug up among the ruins of their towns.

In the fifth century B.C., Rome was a small city-state like Athens, but the Romans had a much greater talent for government and politics than the Greeks. Their state grew bigger and more powerful as time went on, until it became a mighty empire that stretched all the way from England to Egypt and from Spain to Southern Russia. Although they had conquered the Greeks as early as the second century B.C., the Romans always had a great respect for Greek art, so that many of their own painters were influenced by the Greeks.

If we put these Roman pictures together with some of the Greek vases, they help to give us a better notion of the lost masterpieces of Greek wall painting. In figure 13 you see such a Roman mural, taken from a house in the small Italian town of Boscoreale, near Naples. It was done less than a hundred years before the birth of Christ and is so large that the figures in it are just about life-size. Still, it will remind you a good deal of the young women on the vase in figure 10, which in reality are only a few inches tall.

The Roman lady still has something of the idealized beauty that we find in the Greek picture, even though she is not nearly as graceful. At the same time, she seems more real than the Greek women, and not only because of the rich color and the careful shading. Her face, with its strong nose, looks as if it might be a portrait, and the little girl behind the chair could be her daughter. The Roman painter often combined the real and the ideal in this fashion. It is hard to say how much they took from the Greeks and how much they invented, but in any case they are important to us because through their work the Greek style of painting was kept alive so that it could be handed on to the artists of the Christian era.

20

STOP

13. LADY MUSICIAN AND YOUNG GIRL. Roman wall painting from Boscoreale. First century B.C., Metropolitan Museum of Art

THE MIDDLE AGES

WHEN WE THINK of the many countries and the different kinds of people that came under Roman rule, we cannot help wondering how the Romans ever managed to hold their empire together. It must have been an almost impossible task. Fortunately, the Romans were too wise to rely on military force alone. After they had conquered a country, they made the people into "Romans" of a sort by teaching them Roman ways and even allowing them to become Roman citizens, with rights and duties fixed by law. There was one thing, however, that the Romans failed to do: they did not give the people within the Empire a common religious faith. The official Roman religion was like that of the Greeks, but the Romans never insisted that everybody had to accept it. All they required was a formal sacrifice every year to the emperor, who was to them a kind of hero-god, like the Greek Hercules. For the rest, the Greek gods, the Egyptian gods, and all the other local gods were allowed to compete with each other; and since there were so many of them, nobody really knew *what* to believe in.

Such confusion was all very well as long as the empire was stable and peaceful, but when things began to go badly people felt a great need for the comfort and assurance that comes from a strong faith. It was then that they turned to the followers of Jesus Christ, the group most zealous in offering such a faith to the rest of the world. By the time the Empire was ready to collapse, Christianity had won out over all the other religions, and the Christian Church was well established.

Jesus Christ was born among the Jews, who had long believed in a single God while their neighbors worshipped many different gods. God, as the Jews thought of Him, was all-powerful; He had created the entire world and ruled over everything. All men were His children, but He had a special concern for the Jews, His chosen people, to whom He had made known His will in the form of laws or commandments. These laws, written down in the Old Testament, told men exactly how to behave towards each other if they wanted to lead good and worthwhile lives. This was a great and new concept: that God is just, and that the only way to please Him is by obeying His commandments.

Jesus, too, accepted the laws of the Old Testament. But He said that to observe these laws was less important than to love God, because God was filled with kindness and mercy for all men, even those who broke His laws. Jesus also believed that we must be as kind and forgiving to other people as God is to us. His own life, and His death on the cross, as told in the Gospels of the New Testament, give us a perfect example of what He meant by this. To His followers, Jesus was the Son of God, the Saviour whose coming had been predicted by the Prophets in the Old Testament. They believed that God had sent Him in order to redeem mankind; that those who placed their trust in Christ would rise after death and live forever in Paradise; and that God offered this hope not only to the Jews but to all races and nations, to rich and poor alike.

This last part of their faith explains why the followers of Jesus were so eager to spread their message everywhere. Soon after His death, they went to different parts of the Roman Empire. There they taught the new religion and formed the earliest Christian congregations, or Churches. The most important Church was in Rome; and there, too, we find the first pictures by Christian artists. They were painted on the walls of long underground passages called catacombs, where the Early Christians buried their dead. Figure 14 shows you the remains of a ceiling decoration from such a catacomb, done about two centuries after the death of Christ. Its style is borrowed from Roman painting, but the figures in it are simpler and more sketchy; they also look a bit stiff, and seem to cling to the white background. Obviously, our artist was not much interested in modeling or foreshortening.

We can tell from this that the Early Christians even then had an outlook on life quite different from that of the believers in the Roman religion. Their thoughts were centered on the Saviour and on the life hereafter, rather than on their own strength or on the glories of this earth. Thus the beauty and power of the human body, which had been so important in Greek and Roman art, no longer held much meaning for them; instead, they wanted pictures that would show the power and glory of Christ, and tell of His mission on earth.

The Early Christian painter could not do this directly. He could only hint at it by using symbols— that is, figures or signs that stand for something which we cannot see. The picture in the middle of the ceiling is such a symbol; it shows a shepherd and his flock, but it stands for Christ, the Good Shepherd of men's souls. Since everything depends on Christ, the other scenes are arranged around this center like the spokes of a wheel. They form a big cross, the simplest and most

23

14. PAINTED CEILING from the Catacomb of Saints Peter and
Marcellinus. Rome, early third century

general symbol of the new faith. The standing figures represent the members of the Church, with their hands raised in prayer, pleading for help from above. In the four half-circles our artist tells the story of Jonah, from the Old Testament. Jonah had gone on a boat against the wishes of God, so the sailors threw him into the sea and a whale swallowed him. You see this in the scene on the left (the whale is shown as a kind of sea monster). On the right, the whale is letting him out again, because Jonah had prayed to God while he was inside the big fish. At the bottom, he is back on dry land, meditating about the mercy of God.

To the Early Christians, this story meant that they, too, would rise from the dead through the power of God, just as Jonah had risen from the whale. And they needed to be reassured, for they were having quite a hard time themselves. Still, more and more people joined them, so that in the fourth century even the emperors were Christians. Not long after this, Christianity became the official religion of the Roman Empire, and when that happened Christian art, too, began to take on a more official look. But by this time the western part of the Empire was falling to pieces, and the capital had been moved from Rome to Byzantium, in eastern Greece. The official Christian style of painting has been called Byzantine after that city, whose modern name is Istanbul.

This style of painting lived on, without any really vital or important changes, for

15. MADONNA AND CHILD from the Catacomb of Priscilla. Rome, third century

a very long time. The Byzantine *Madonna* in figure 16—that is, the Virgin Mary with her son, the Infant Christ—probably dates from around 1200, but it would be much the same if it had been painted a few centuries earlier or later. It is done on a wooden panel, like the portrait of the boy in figure 12, and the subject may remind you of the lady with the little girl in figure 13, but these comparisons only show us how different it is from Roman or even Early Christian painting. The Byzantine artist did not think of the Madonna as anything like an ordinary, human mother. To him she was the Queen of Heaven, far removed from everyday life and beautiful beyond any man's imagination. And he has painted her the way he *felt* about her: not as a woman of flesh and blood, made up of solid, round forms, but an ideal figure bathed in the golden light of heaven.

If we now look left at figure 15, an Early

16. MADONNA AND CHILD ENTHRONED. Byzantine, about 1200. National Gallery of Art, Washington D. C.

17. Page from the Book of Durrow. Irish, seventh century. Trinity College, Dublin

18. Saint Matthew from the Gospel Book of Charlemagne. About 800. Museum, Vienna

Christian *Madonna* from the wall of a catacomb, we can see that it stands about halfway between the Roman lady and the Byzantine *Madonna*. It is much more human than the later picture, but the dark, staring eyes and the stiffness of the body tell us that we are looking at something sacred and symbolic. Subjects like this were repeated over and over again, and each time they became a little less natural as one painter copied from another, until at last they reached the frozen, super-human majesty of the Byzantine style.

THE EARLIER MIDDLE AGES IN THE WEST

Meanwhile, western Europe had been invaded by warlike tribes from the north and east. They conquered the Roman armies and made independent local kingdoms of the various provinces of the Empire, mixing through intermarriage with the people whom they found there. The nations of western Europe as we know them today—the English, the French, and the rest—all got their start in this melting pot. But first the tribes had to be taught about Roman civilization and about Christianity. They were now the heirs of everything that had been achieved by the older nations around the Mediterranean Sea, and there was a great deal they had to learn.

During this troubled time, which lasted for many centuries, the Church was the only stable institution that remained in western Europe. The task of spreading both faith and education fell to the monks—devoted religious men who lived together under strict discipline in

26

19. First page of the GOSPEL OF LUKE. French, about 1000. Pierpont Morgan Library, New York

special communities. The monks, however, were not only priests and teachers. From the fifth to the twelfth century—that is, for most of the period we know as the Middle Ages—they were also the leading artists and craftsmen.

In those days almost every monastery had a workshop for making copies of the Bible and other books. This was done by hand, since printing had not yet been invented. The monks did not even know about paper; they wrote on vellum, a material made from the skin of calves, which was much more expensive but also a great deal tougher. Medieval books—or manuscripts, as they are usually called—were meant to last for a long time, and many of them are still in fine shape. The writing shops also included painters whose job it was to illuminate —to "brighten"—the manuscripts with pictures and ornament. These miniatures (from "minium," a red pigment) were done with marvelous care. For a long time they were the most important kind of medieval painting, and the best of them can stand comparison with any mural or panel picture.

It is not surprising that the monks took manuscript painting so seriously. After all, their faith was based on the Bible, which to many people is still simply "the Book." Since it contained the word of God, every copy of it was sacred, and to illuminate it, to make it as beautiful as possible, was a way of worshipping God. Perhaps this idea will help us under-stand the manuscript page in figure 17, from the *Book of Durrow*, which was done by Irish monks in the seventh century. The words that go with this picture are those of the Gospels —the life of Christ written by the four Evangelists, Matthew, Mark, Luke, and John—but our artist has not tried to illustrate the sacred story. Instead, he has brightened it up with a wonderful piece of ornament. These interlaced bands and weird, band-like animals do not come from Early Christian art; they are borrowed from the native art of the tribes that had just settled in western Europe. And yet, the picture has a Christian meaning. You will notice that it is made up of a circle with a small cross in the center, with a wide frame around it.

20. THE BUILDING OF THE TOWER OF BABEL. Painting in the Church of St. Savin. French, twelfth century

21. OLD TESTAMENT KING. Detail from a Stained Glass Window. German, about
1300. Metropolitan Museum of Art, New York

This is our artist's way of showing the contrast between two different worlds: the frame, with its fighting monsters, stands for the cruel, dark world of the pagans, the unbelievers; while the circle is a symbol of the world under Christ.

Our next miniature (figure 18) was painted around 800 A.D., at the time of Charlemagne, the first medieval emperor, who ruled over France, Germany, and most of Italy. Charlemagne not only revived the idea of the Roman Empire in the West; he also wanted his people to learn everything they could about Roman civilization and about Early Christian art (because that, too, came from Rome). In the pictures of Charlemagne's own Gospel Book, there are no interlacing bands and tangled-up animals. Instead, we find the four Evangelists, carefully copied from Early Christian manuscripts. The one you see in figure 18 is Saint Matthew. Everything about him—the powerful body, the bold head, and especially the use of shading and foreshortening—reminds us of Roman art. We might well mistake him for something painted many centuries earlier, if it weren't for the halo behind his head, which is a symbol to tell us that he is no ordinary author but a man filled with the spirit of God. (If you turn back to the Byzantine Madonna and Child in figure 16, you will see that they also possess halos.)

But the Roman spirit of Charlemagne's time did not last. His empire was split up among his heirs, and reverted to being pretty much of a local power, and in art, too, the native ornamental style of interlacing bands and animal forms came back after a few years. However, the painters also remembered what they had learned under Charlemagne—how to draw human figures and tell stories with pictures. So they began to combine the two styles into one. The result was a great new style, the so-called Romanesque, which flowered in the eleventh and twelfth centuries. Despite its name, it is not at all Roman in spirit, although many of its forms are of Roman origin.

Figure 19 shows you a fine early example of Romanesque painting. It is the first page of the Gospel of Luke, from a manuscript illuminated in a French monastery soon after the year 1000 A.D. Look at the marvelous way the ornament, the text, and the illustrations are woven together here! There is so much to see that we hardly know where to start. The wide frame reminds us of the one from the *Book of Durrow*, but the interlacing bands have sprouted leaves and flowers, and the animals are less fierce and easier to recognize. At the top and bottom, we even have little hunting scenes. The large shape in the middle of the page is the initial letter "Q", again outlined with plant and animal forms. It frames a scene from the Gospel: the angel Gabriel announcing the birth of Saint John the Baptist to Zacharias. In the tail of the "Q" we see another sacred story, the birth of Christ.

These pictures show us that the Romanesque painter was quite familiar with the "official" Christian style of Byzantine art and respected its authority. When he designed the ornament of the frame, he simply invented his patterns as he went along, but for the sacred stories of the Bible he did not trust his own imagination. They had to be illustrated "correctly"—that is, the way they had been done by earlier artists—otherwise people might not recognize them. But if our artist has used Byzantine pictures as his models, he has not copied them very exactly. While his figures have a good deal in common with the Byzantine *Madonna* on page 25, they are much more forceful and expressive. In fact, they seem to be full of the same kind of energy and excitement as the plant and animal forms of the frame. This is what makes them Romanesque, and it also explains why the design of the whole page hangs together so well, despite its many different elements.

The story-telling power of the Romanesque style can be seen even better in our next picture (figure 20), a mural of the twelfth century from St. Savin in France. There used to be a great many such wall

22. DAVID AND GOLIATH. Prayerbook of Philippe le Bel. French, 1295. National Library, Paris

23. Giotto. Lamentation over Christ. 1305–6. From the Arena Chapel, Padua, Italy

paintings in the churches of this period, but few of them have survived intact. The subject here is the story of the Tower of Babel, from the Old Testament. This tower was to be a real skyscraper. The people who built it wanted to reach all the way up to heaven, to show that they were just as powerful as God. But they never finished it, because God suddenly made each of them speak a different language, so they could no longer understand each other. In our picture, the men on the right, led by the giant Nimrod, are carrying stone blocks for the masons on the tower. On the left you see God warning them to stop. The artist has put all this into a long, narrow strip, so that we follow the story as our eyes move back and forth across the picture, that perhaps will remind you of the "strip pictures" of ancient Egypt (figure 6). The Romanesque painter, too, shows us what he knows, not what he sees, but how intensely and dramatically he tells his story. In the Egyptian painting, all the figures seem to be standing still. Here, every line is in motion; people are beckoning to each other, straining under the load of the stones, arguing with God. We know right away that this is a great test of strength between ambitious men and their Creator, and we share the excitement the artist must have felt when he painted the picture.

THE RISE OF THE TOWNS: GOTHIC ART

DURING the earlier Middle Ages, the towns left over from the time of the Roman Empire were almost deserted, and those that had been newly founded remained small and quite unimportant. Most of the people lived in the open country, where they farmed the land belonging to the monasteries or the nobles. But from the twelfth century on, the towns began to grow again. More and more people left the countryside to become "burghers," free town-dwellers no longer bound to the land-owning overlords. This brought about a great change in medieval life. The burghers were skilled craftsmen and enterprising traders, so that the towns soon became the centers of wealth, and of art and learning as well. Also, city life made people more independent and practical-minded. It opened them up to all sorts of new ideas, and gave them a greater interest in the world around them.

Out of this new spirit came a new style in art called the Gothic. It started in France about 1150 A.D. and spread from there to all the other countries of the Western world. The miniature in figure 22, from a prayerbook dated 1295 A.D., will show you how very different Gothic painting is from Romanesque. It was done by a burgher, a professional manuscript painter in the city of Paris, rather than by a monk. The subject is the famous Old Testament story of the victory of David over the Philistine Goliath, but our artist has treated it as if it had happened in his own lifetime. The giant Goliath, in the center, and King Saul, on the left, are wearing the armor of medieval knights. What really surprises us, however, is the new interest in shading, which gives all the forms a softer, more natural look. While our picture as a whole has little depth, there is enough modeling here to lift the figures away from the flat pattern of the background, and the way their feet overlap the frame shows us that they are meant to be *in front of* the page, not just *on* it.

Another kind of painting that flourished in Gothic times was done on small pieces of colored glass, which were cut to shape and then fitted together with lead frames into large stained glass windows. The Old Testament king in figure 21 is a detail from such a window, made in Germany around the year 1300 A.D. Here you see the same soft, loopy folds of drapery as in the miniature of David and Goliath, but the difficult and limited technique of

32

24. Simone Martini. CHRIST CARRYING THE CROSS. About 1340. Louvre Museum, Paris

this art has made modeling almost impossible. Perhaps we should not think of stained glass windows as pictures at all; they are really transparent screens whose beauty depends on the marvelously rich and brilliant color patterns. These windows were an essential part of Gothic architecture. In France, England, and Germany they reached such great size that the churches began to look like glass buildings, and there was little space left for murals.

Italy alone was an exception to this rule. There the churches kept their solid walls, and mural painting continued to be a great art for many centuries. But the Italians were different from the nations to the north in other ways as well. They had never quite forgotten that they were the heirs of the Romans and Early Christians, and they knew much more about city life. Italy had wealthy and powerful medieval towns earlier than any other country, so that we need not be surprised to meet a particularly bold and "modern" spirit among Italian Gothic painters. The greatest of them all was Giotto, who was born in the city of Florence in 1266. He is the first painter in history who is as much admired today as he was during his own lifetime. We know that his works were considered something new and wonderful then; and since a good many of them have come down to us, we can find out for ourselves why he became so famous. Looking at his *Lamentation over Christ* (figure 23), which is one of a series of murals in a private chapel in Padua, we feel right away that it must be a large picture, not a miniature from some manuscript. This has little to do with the actual size—it's the bigness of the shapes that makes the painting seem so large. There is no fussy detail in these strong and simple figures. Their weight and roundness almost make them look like great rocks. We call such figures monumental, because they remind us of a stone monument, firmly set in place for all time.

Yet Giotto's people are full of human feeling. We share their sorrow over the death of Christ, whether we look at the weeping angels in the sky or at the mourners below. Through their gestures, and the expressions on their faces, they speak to us so clearly and simply that we ourselves become part of the scene. But there is something else that makes the *Lamentation* such a powerful work of art: its composition—by which we mean the way the figures and other forms are arranged inside the frame. When we look at story-telling pictures like the Romanesque mural or the Gothic miniature, our eye travels from one detail to the next. In the *Lamentation*, on the other hand, the large, simple forms and the strong grouping of the figures allow us to see the entire scene at one glance. Giotto has composed it the way a great stage director would put on a dramatic play in the theater. Even the scenery makes us think of a stage set; it leaves just enough room for the bulky figures, but the background looks flat. If we follow the foreshortened right arm of the Saint John, in the center, we can measure the actual depth of the "stage."

Before Giotto, Italian painting had been closely tied to the Byzantine style. If you compare his work with the Byzantine *Madonna* in figure 16, you will understand why he came to be remembered as the man who led Italian art back to natural forms. The painters of Siena,

34

25. Paul of Limburg and brothers. FEBRUARY. From the "Very Rich Book of Hours of the Duke of Berry."
About 1415. Condé Museum, Chantilly

26. Melchior Broederlam. WING OF AN ALTAR PANEL.
About 1395. Museum, Dijon

a town not far from Florence, had a similar aim but went about it another way. They "unfroze" the Byzantine style, so that it became more lively and realistic. Among the best was Simone Martini, who painted the small wooden panel of *Christ Carrying the Cross* (figure 24). The picture is done in tempera, a technique used for both miniatures and panels (the colors are mixed with egg yolk and water, making a thin, smooth paint that dries to a tough enamel-like film). The fine detail and the brilliant colors give this kind of painting a jewel-like quality very different from fresco. Some of Simone's figures still remind us of Byzantine art, while others show the influence of Giotto in their bulk and expressiveness. Giotto's sense of drama is missing, to be sure, but Simone has a wonderful eye for all the little touches that bring the scene to life, such as the costumes or the pushing and pulling of people in a crowd, so that in some ways he comes even closer to reality. Notice how he has struggled to give depth to his painting: he shows us not only the people pouring out of the city in the background, but the city itself. The foreshortened view is a bit awkward still, but at least the picture space is no longer limited to a narrow foreground stage.

Simone Martini also became an important link between Italy and Northern Europe. He spent some years in the south of France, where he came to know French Gothic art while the French learned about the new Italian style from him. By the end of the fourteenth century, exchanges of this kind had become so frequent that there was no longer much of a difference between the Italian and the Northern painters. They all worked in a style which we often call "International Gothic" in order to stress their similarity of outlook.

The next three pictures date from this period, which lasted only until about 1420. The panel in figure 26 was painted in the 1390's by Melchior Broederlam for his patron, the Duke of Burgundy. It is one of a pair of wings to fit an altar shrine (this explains its odd shape). On the left side, which shows the Christ Child being presented to the High Priest in the Temple, we see how much Broederlam has learned from the Italians about architectural space in painting. His temple looks a bit unreal, as if it were a sort of cage built around the figures, yet it has a good deal of depth. There is Italian influence, too, in the heavy-set figures. The soft, flowing folds of the costumes, on the other hand, remind us of the *David and*

Goliath miniature, except that they are richer and more complicated. Such ample garments were popular among the artists of that time, since they made the figures look bulkier. On the right we see the Holy Family—Mary, Joseph, and the Infant Christ—fleeing into Egypt. The softly shaded rocky slopes, the trees and flowers done with such loving care, show us how important landscape painting has become by now. For Broederlam, every detail of the natural world was worth looking at—plants, animals, and people; his charming donkey is certainly painted from life, and the Joseph makes us think of a rough, simple farmer.

The same interest in nature and the everyday world is found in the *Very Rich Book of Hours*, the finest illuminated manuscript of the International Style. It was painted around 1415 by Paul of Limburg and his two brothers for the Duke of Berry, one of the great noblemen of France. Figure 25 shows the calendar for the month of February and the miniature that goes with it, telling us about country life in mid-winter. And what a complete and delightful picture it is! We can almost feel the cold in the still, clear air as we watch the birds scratching for feed in the barnyard, the farmhands warming themselves at the fire, or the peasant driving his donkey towards the village among the snowy hills in the distance.

The Birth of Christ (figure 27) was done in 1423 as part of a large altarpiece, by Gentile da Fabriano, an Italian who must have known such Northern painters as Broederlam and the Limburg brothers. The soft shading, the loopy folds of drapery, the carefully studied animals and plants—all these are familiar to us by now; what really interests us about this panel is the lighting. In the pictures we have seen so far, we could never tell what time of day it was, or what kind of light the artist had in mind. Here for the first time we have a real night scene, and we know exactly where the light is coming from. Its main source is the Christ Child himself. He had long been called "the light of the world," but until now nobody had painted this divine light as if it were a warm little campfire. Only in the years around 1400 did artists begin to realize that light is something separate from form and color and perhaps even more important, since the way we see things depends on how the light strikes them. You will read about this discovery in the next chapter.

27. Gentile da Fabriano. THE BIRTH OF CHRIST. 1423. From an Altar in the Uffizi Gallery, Florence

EXPLORERS AND DISCOVERERS

IT IS ALWAYS HARD TO ESTABLISH with any certainty the exact moment when something new began. The calendar may tell us that March 21 is the first day of spring, but if we are asked about the *real* start of the new season we cannot pin it down as neatly as that. It is just as hard for us to say when the modern age began. We do know, however, that the Middle Ages came to an end between the fourteenth and the sixteenth centuries—in some places this happened much sooner than in others—and that the Western world entered a new and vital era called the Renaissance. Gothic art, with its growing interest in nature and its more human approach to religious stories, has shown us that people's outlook on life was beginning to change even earlier.

By about 1420, this curiosity about animals, plants, and people had become a tremendous urge to explore the whole world and everything in it. People were less and less willing

28. Hubert or Jan van Eyck. THE BAPTISM OF CHRIST, from a Book of Hours. About 1416–20. Museo Civico, Turin

29. Hubert or Jan van Eyck. THE CRUCIFIXION and THE LAST JUDGMENT. About 1420. Metropolitan Museum of Art

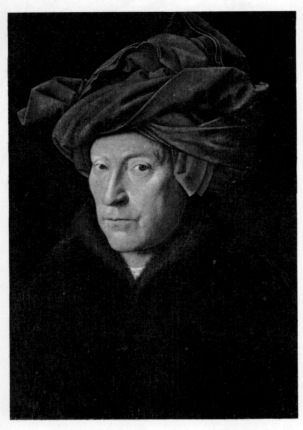

30. Jan van Eyck. The Man in the Red Turban. 1433. National Gallery, London

to take things on faith; they wanted to ask their own questions and look for themselves. Bold seafarers set out for unknown lands and came back with reports that helped to fill in the blank spots on the map. Columbus, who discovered America in 1492, was one of these. Other men explored the field of mechanics and invented important new techniques, such as printing (about 1450) which made books so cheap that many more people could afford them than before. And the artists, too, turned into explorers. Simply by taking a fresh look at things, they discovered that the world around them was full of beauties and wonders that no one had been aware of before. In fact, they often knew more about the workings of nature than the scientists of their day, because they had learned how to use their eyes, while the scientists still relied on medieval book-learning.

LATE GOTHIC ART

WHILE both the Italian and the Northern painters broke away from the International Style at the same time, they did not do it in the same way. That is the reason we use different names for their work. Italian fifteenth-century art is called "Early Renaissance"; that of the Northern countries "Late Gothic"—even though the two styles have a good many things in common. Late Gothic painting had its start in the wealthy towns of Flanders (or Belgium, as it is called today). The great masters of Bruges and Brussels were so famous that the new style was known all over Europe simply as "Flemish." The earliest of these great discoverers were the brothers Hubert and Jan van Eyck. One or the other of the two probably did the miniature of the Baptism of Christ (figure 28). It was painted only a year or two after the *Very Rich Book of Hours*, and yet what a difference there is if we compare it with the February landscape of figure 25. The Limburg brothers were more interested in all the charming details they had collected than in the scene as a whole; because of this, their picture makes us think not of a real landscape but of a miniature model where everything is just as small as they have painted it. In *The Baptism of Christ*, on the contrary, we are shown a piece of the real world, as if a window had been cut into the page. If we could wander about in this landscape, we would find everything to be life-size, not scaled down to miniature.

31. Roger van der Weyden. CHRIST APPEARING TO HIS MOTHER. About 1440. Metropolitan Museum of Art

And why are we so convinced of this? Because the van Eycks had made a great discovery: what we see in real life depends on how the light is picked up by the things we are looking at, and also on the air that is between these things and ourselves. Some surfaces, such as rocks or trees, swallow up most of the light that hits them, while others make it bounce back, like a mirror. In our picture, the calm water of the river acts in this way—it reflects not only the light of the sky but the trees and the castle along the bank. Earlier artists had not bothered with mirror images. The van Eycks, on the other hand, looked upon them as an important test of the painter's power: if you could show the difference between a reflection and the real thing in your pictures, then you had learned all there was to know about light.

What the van Eycks found out about air was equally new and important. We all know that in foggy weather the air sometimes gets so "thick" that we can see only a few feet ahead. But the air is never completely clear. Even on the brightest of days it acts like a hazy screen between us and the things we are looking at; the farther away these things are, the dimmer and greyer they seem. The van Eycks were the first painters to understand this clearly.

In *The Baptism of Christ*, every form is both "air-conditioned" and "light-conditioned," so that all the details fall into place just as they do in nature. What holds the scene together, then, and makes it so different from all the pictures we have seen before, is a new kind of order based on the behavior of light and air. It is a very strict order, which works only if the artist sticks to it in every detail. If he makes any exceptions, for the sake of story-telling, or symbolic meaning, or decoration, his picture will no longer look like a window into the natural world. The van Eycks knew this, too; they have put Christ and Saint John in the best spot they could find, but the figures are still so small that we hardly notice them in the wide and wonderful landscape.

Imaginary windows don't fit very well on a manuscript page, because the letters and the ornament keep telling us that the page is something flat and white, and that we must not *try* to look through it. No wonder the van Eycks soon switched to panel pictures, where they could "paint away" the entire surface inside the frame. You will see how successful they were in this if you turn to the two small pictures of figure 29. These are painted in a complicated new technique the van Eycks had helped to develop; we still don't know exactly how they did it, but apparently they used one or more coats of very thin oil paint on top of tempera. The oil paint would let the colors underneath shine through, producing softer shades and a richer blending of tones than one could get from tempera alone. The tall and narrow shape of the panels indicates that they are the wings of a small altar; they probably flanked a larger center panel which has been lost.

The left-hand wing shows the Crucifixion. We seem to be looking down at the scene, as if we were watching it from a position in mid-air. This was the only way the van Eycks could tell the story of the Crucifixion as clearly as they wanted to, but without breaking the rules that made a window out of the picture. If they had put us down on the ground among

32. Southern French Master. The Avignon Pieta. About 1470. Louvre Museum, Paris

the bystanders, they would have had to make the figures in the foreground so large that our view would have been cut off.

Since this is a color plate, you can see even better than before how completely the van Eycks have mastered the light and air of the natural world. Notice how the colors get paler in the distance until we can no longer tell where the earth leaves off and the sky begins. Perhaps it will have struck you that despite the milling crowds of people there is hardly any drama or action in the picture. The van Eycks seem to have paid just as much attention to all the things that are *not* part of the story—the rocks on the ground, the details of the costumes, the landscape behind the crosses—as to the human figures. But this does not mean that they were any less religious than the painters of the Middle Ages. If you could ask them about it, they would probably say that God had created not only man but the rest of the natural world as well; why then should a pebble or a blade of grass be less of a miracle, less worthy of our respect, than man himself?

43

33. The Master of Moulins. A Young Princess. About 1490. Collection Robert Lehman, New York

While the story of the Crucifixion could be told in terms of the natural world, the subject of the right-hand wing had to be made up entirely from the artist's imagination. It is the Last Judgment: at the end of time, so the prophecy goes, all the dead will rise from their graves to have their deeds judged by God. We can see them coming out of the ground and the ocean in the middle of the picture. Above them is the Lord, surrounded by the blessed souls who are being admitted to everlasting life in Paradise. Down below, the sinners who have been condemned to living death in Hell are being tortured by devilish monsters. Into this Hell, which has the awful reality of a nightmare, the van Eycks have poured all the violent action, all the expressiveness they seem to avoid everywhere else. Here we see that the new painting rules can be applied even to a subject as "un-natural" as this; far from stifling the artist's imagination, they only help him to make these fantastic demons more believable, and the pains of the damned more heart-rending, than ever before.

In medieval painting there had been no real portraits, because nobody had thought it worthwhile to record the things that make one person look different from another. Now, in the fifteenth century, people wanted portraits they could recognize, and the painters learned very quickly how to do likenesses of this kind. The *Man in the Red Turban* (figure 30) was done by Jan van Eyck in 1433. We do not know the sitter's name, but it may very well be the artist himself (there is a slight strain about the eyes, as if the man were gazing into a mirror). Here again we marvel at the rich play of light and shade, which gives us the "feel" of every surface, from the stubble of beard on the chin to the crinkly fabric of the turban. Yet, strangely enough, we learn very little about the character of this man; his face is as calm, as undisturbed by thoughts or feelings, as the landscape in *The Baptism of Christ*.

The next picture (figure 31) dates from about 1440. It is the work of another great Flemish master, Roger van der Weyden, who had been strongly influenced by the discoveries of the van Eycks. Roger's main concern, however, was not the world around us but the world within us—he was the great explorer of human feeling in religious art. The panel shows Christ appearing to his mother after he had risen from the grave. The Virgin Mary has been reading her prayer book; suddenly, she feels the presence of her son and turns her grief-stricken face towards him, while he raises his hands as if to reassure her. There is an air of deep sadness and suffering about these two figures that immediately touches our heart, because their feelings seem as real to us as the painted architecture or the fine, airy landscape in the background. The

34. Jerome Bosch. THE SHIP OF FOOLS. About 1500. Louvre Museum, Paris

setting may strike you at first as rather too elaborate, but if you study it more closely you will find that almost every detail has a meaning related to the main figures: the stone carvings on the arched portal tell us about other events in the life of the Virgin, and in the distance we see Christ leaving his tomb while the soldiers on guard are asleep. This is perhaps the most astonishing thing about Late Gothic painting—how the natural world is made to contain the world of the spirit in such a way that the two actually become one.

It was Roger who made the new Flemish style known all over Northern Europe. Among the countless artists from neighboring countries who felt his influence there was a Frenchman whose name has been forgotten; in fact, we know only a single work by his hand, but that picture, painted in the years around 1470, is one of the most famous in all of Late Gothic painting (figure 32). It is known as *The Avignon Pietà*, since it was found near the city of Avignon, in the south of France. "Pietà" is the Italian word for "pity," but it also has come to mean the image of the dead Christ in the lap of his mother. In our picture the Madonna is flanked by Saint John and Saint Mary Magdalene. The figure kneeling in prayer on the left is a portrait of the man who ordered the painting.

35. Masaccio. THE HOLY TRINITY. About 1427.
Church of Santa Maria Novella, Florence

The *Pietà* does not tell a story; it is meant, rather, to make us share the silent grief of the Virgin by reminding us that a younger and happier Madonna once held the Infant Christ on her lap in much the same way. There are many things in our picture that recall Roger van der Weyden, but its design is very much simpler, and in this simplicity lies its strength. It has a "bigness" about it that makes us think of Giotto. And we may not be altogether wrong: Avignon is closer to Italy than to Flanders, so that our master might well have been touched by Italian art even though his *Pietà* remains entirely Late Gothic in feeling.

At the end of the century, the most important French painter was again an artist for whom we have no certain name; we call him the "Master of Moulins." The young princess (figure 33) whose picture he painted about 1490 could not have been more than ten

36. Fra Angelico and Fra Filippo Lippi. THE ADORATION OF THE MAGI.
About 1445. National Gallery of Art, Washington, D. C. (Kress Collection)

years old. We can tell by her elegant costume and by the castle in the background that she must be somebody important. Fortunately, our painter has not been overawed by her high rank; he shows her as a delicate and gentle little girl, perhaps a bit too serious for one so young. Or could it be that the hint of sadness in her face is just another echo of the style of Roger van der Weyden?

47

Our next picture (figure 34) was painted by Jerome Bosch, an extraordinary Dutch master who seems closer to the van Eycks than to Roger van der Weyden. Its soft, airy background will remind you of *The Baptism of Christ*, and the jerky gestures and excited expressions of the figures have something in common with the violent Hell scene of *The Last Judgment*. Bosch, too, shows us a kind of hell, but it is a hell of man's own making. His painting was inspired by a popular book, *The Ship of Fools*. It tells us that the world is full of silly people whose only aim is to have a good time. Instead of preparing for the day when God will judge their deeds on earth, they float through life as if it were a pleasure trip. And yet they don't seem at all happy, despite their frantic merry-making: in their greed they overeat, get drunk, and fight among themselves, while their ship is drifting towards dangerous waters. We can be quite sure that the journey will come to no good end.

THE EARLY RENAISSANCE IN ITALY

WE MAY be amused by the Punch-and-Judy antics of Bosch's figures, but actually they show us a grim, even hopeless, view of human nature and of man's place in the world. As the Middle Ages came to an end in Northern Europe, there were many people who felt the way Bosch did—lost, frightened, longing for a new faith to take the place of the old. But in Italy this mood was not so general. In fact, many Italians welcomed the new era as a rebirth, for that is what the word "Renaissance" means, and they were the ones who coined it. It was, they said, the rebirth of those powers of the human mind that had created the glories of Greece and Rome. The thousand years since the death of Classical Antiquity they called the "Middle Ages," meaning "the time in-between" when little of real importance had been done in the arts. And for the style that had been brought into Italy from the North they invented the insulting label "Gothic," because they disliked it so. (The Goths were one of the tribes that had helped to destroy the Roman Empire in Early Christian times.) Today we no longer despise the art of the Middle Ages or look down on Gothic art as inferior, although we still employ the same designations.

Naturally, of course, the Italians did not try to turn themselves into Classical Romans pure and simple. They certainly had no idea of giving up the Christian faith. Still, they believed that we ought to rely more on ourselves, instead of depending on God for everything. "Since the Lord has given us such remarkable powers of mind, and such a beautiful world to live in," they asked, "is it not our duty to make full use of these gifts?" The Ancients, they felt, had in many ways done a better job of this than anybody else, so there was a lot to be learned from them. But they always thought of themselves as the rivals of Classical Antiquity, not as mere imitators; they took from it what they needed, and left the rest alone.

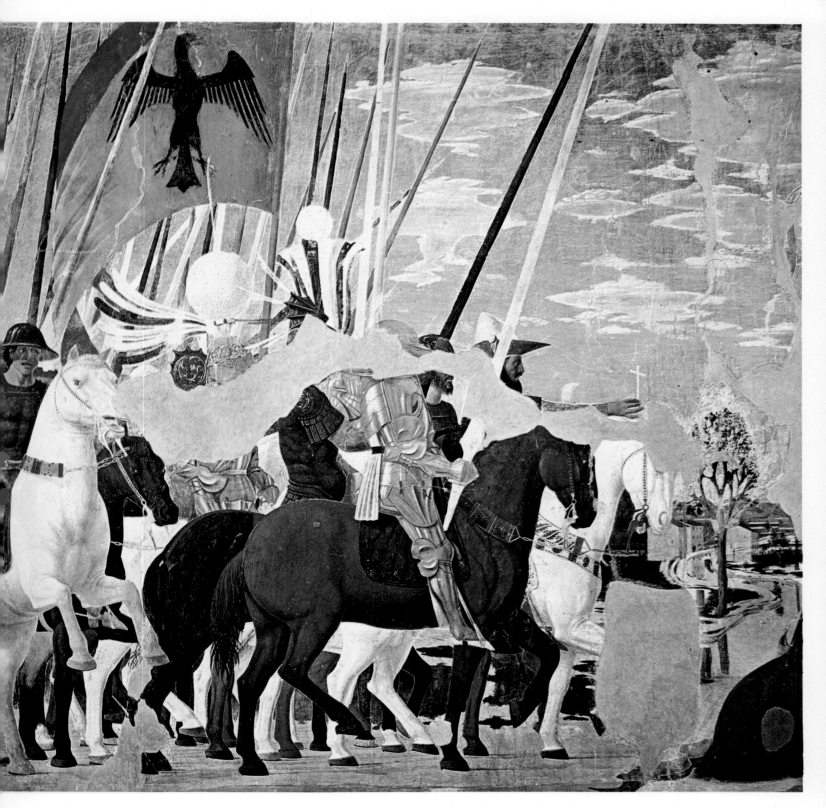

37. Piero della Francesca. THE BATTLE OF CONSTANTINE (detail). About 1460. Church of San Francesco, Arezzo, Italy

Florence, the home town of Giotto, can be considered the birthplace of Renaissance art. In the field of painting, the new style began and evolved from the work of Masaccio, a youthful genius who died about 1428 when he was barely twenty-eight years old. We have only a few paintings by his hand, but these are quite enough to show us that he was an even bolder explorer than were the van Eycks. The fresco of *The Holy Trinity with Saint John and Saint Mary* (figure 35), which he painted about 1427,

49

38. Piero della Francesca. Illustration from "De Prospectiva Pingendi"

39. ANCIENT STATUE OF A FLEEING WARRIOR. Uffizi Gallery, Florence

owes nothing to the International Style; we can tell from the monumental, bulky figures, and the "bigness" of the design as a whole, that Masaccio has gone back a full hundred years to pick up the style of Giotto. And yet we find a great difference between the two: Giotto's figures remind us of carved stones, while Masaccio's seem to be made of flesh and blood. But then Giotto was, after all, a medieval artist. When he painted a human figure, he thought only of what it would tell us, or how it would make us feel; he was not interested in putting it together the way such figures are put together in real life. Masaccio, on the other hand, tried to do exactly that. We might say that he wanted to do Giotto over again, but from nature. You will see what this means if you look, for example, at the Saint John and Saint Mary. Although they are wrapped in heavy cloaks, we can feel the shape of their bodies under the drapery, and this is something we haven't been able to do since we looked at the Roman mural in figure 13. Masaccio had never seen anything like that, but he worked in much the same way as the Ancient painters: he thought of the bodies of his figures first, and then put the clothes on them separately. In order to do that, however, he had to find out how clothes behave—what kinds of folds you get when you pull a cloak around your shoulders, or bunch it over your arm, or let it hang to the floor. This is why the draperies in the *Trinity* fresco have the natural flow of real cloth.

But Masaccio also needed to know about the forms underneath the drapery; and that was very much more difficult, for it meant that he had to relearn everything the Ancients had discovered (and the Middle Ages had forgotten) about the workings of the human body. A look at his Christ on the cross will tell you how amazingly well he succeeded in this. The most remarkable thing about the figure is not just that every bone, every muscle is in the right place; it's the way all these details fit together. Masaccio realized that the body is like a complicated and finely adjusted machine, which will run only if all the parts are in working order. That is why all his figures look so strong and full of energy. If you turn back for a moment to the *Christ* of Roger van der Weyden (figure 31), you will find that there, too, the details are well observed, but the "working order" is missing; the joints seem stiff, the muscles weak, and the whole body makes us think of a wooden puppet dangling from invisible strings instead of firmly standing on the ground.

50

40. Andrea del Castagno. THE VICTORIOUS DAVID. About 1450–1455.
National Gallery of Art, Washington, D.C. (Widener Collection)

41. Andrea Mantegna. THE CRUCIFIXION. 1456–1459. Louvre Museum, Paris

(At least that is what Masaccio would probably have thought.) Late Gothic figures never look as if they could do anything by themselves; Early Renaissance ones do, even when they are just standing still or hanging from a cross.

The *Trinity* fresco also shows us another great discovery. Its architectural background is foreshortened according to a set of rules which we call scientific perspective. Earlier painters had used foreshortening of a sort, too, but they had done so in a hit-or-miss fashion, without any rules to guide them. Only scientific perspective made it possible to get a clear and consistent picture of things in space, since it was based on mathematics and the exact measuring of angles and distances. In themselves, the new rules had nothing to do with art or imagination, and yet they were discovered by artists, rather than by scientists, because the artists of the Early Renaissance were so eager to get a firmer grip on the shapes of the natural world.

While Masaccio's bold new style was greatly admired by his fellow artists, it took some time for his ideas to be fully understood. In many other Florentine pictures we can find echoes of the International Style as late as the middle of the fifteenth century. The round panel in figure 36, begun by Fra Angelico and finished by Fra Filippo Lippi about 1445, is an excellent example of this style. It shows the Magi—the three wise men or kings from the East—kneeling in adoration before the Madonna and Child. They have traveled a long way, accompanied by countless servants and animals, as befits their great wealth. You see this crowd pouring through the city gate on the left, but there seems to be no end to them, for the people coming down the mountain in the background still belong to the same vast train. All this makes a wonderfully gay and colorful scene, crammed with fascinating detail; but we miss the order, the clarity and simplicity of Masaccio. Just take a look at the buildings—their lines are slanted in a curious, mixed-up way, without regard to scientific perspective. And the graceful peacock on the roof of the stable in the middle of the picture is much too big. On the other hand, we can feel the influence of Masaccio in some of the figures, such as the dignified Joseph standing next to the Madonna, or the partially dressed figures by the city gate.

Among the painters who were willing to follow Masaccio all the way, the greatest was certainly Piero della Francesca. In figure 37 you see part of a huge, elaborate fresco cycle he did about 1460 in the town of Arezzo, to the south of Florence. It shows the Roman Emperor Constantine, who has just become a Christian, at the head of his army; he is holding up a small white cross for his pagan enemies to see, and so great is the power of this symbol of faith that they flee without a fight. (They fill the right-hand half of the picture, not shown in our plate.) Piero has not given his soldiers the kind of costumes and arms they actually used in Constantine's day, even though he could have found out about these things by studying Roman art if he had wanted to. Yet every shape in the painting has so much firmness and clarity that we may well compare Piero's style to the finest Classical works of the Ancients. No other painter ever came as close as he did to the monumental spirit of Masaccio.

Perhaps it will help you to understand the secret of Piero's greatness if you take a look at figure 38, which shows you some illustrations from a famous book he wrote on the rules of perspective for painters. While these are really scientific drawings and not meant to be works of art, they do tell us something about how Piero studied the forms he put into his own pictures. At the top you see a cube, viewed in such a way that all of its six sides are foreshortened; this is taken from one of the earlier chapters, which deal with mathematical

53

shapes because they are easier to take apart than the shapes of the natural world. Below, there is the head of a man, seen from the side, from above, and from below. The last two drawings also show the odd outlines you would get if you were to slice through the head at various levels, and the thin straight lines and the numbers help you to line up the three views with each other. If you now turn to *The Battle of Constantine* once more and look at the rearing white horse on the left, for example, you can see that Piero must have studied its shape by this same mathematical method. But Piero was much more than a "scientific" artist. He had a splendid feeling for design and great power of expression, otherwise our picture would not look so vigorously alive. And he also understood the new order of light and air which we first found in the works of the van Eycks. The brisk, clear morning air, the sunlight glistening on the shiny armor—these tell

42. Florentine Master. A Young Lady. About 1460. State Museums, Berlin

us as much as the forms themselves about the sense of adventure, the wonderful self-confidence of the age of "rebirth."

So far we have seen no direct influence of Classical art on the painters of the Early Renaissance. This is not really so strange: while the fifteenth century was well acquainted with Ancient architecture and sculpture, it knew almost nothing about Ancient painting. Still, our painters *did* learn from Classical art, by taking ideas from Ancient sculpture and fitting them into their own work. In figure 40 you see how this could be done. It shows the victorious David, painted on a leather shield by Andrea del Castagno soon after 1450. While such a shield was obviously meant only for display and not for actual fighting, its owner wanted everybody to know that he should face his enemies as bravely as David. In our picture, David has already won out over Goliath, but he is again wielding his sling and challenging all comers. Perhaps you will remember the Gothic miniature (figure 22) where David appears as a mere child who could never have done what he did if his hands had not been guided by the Lord himself. That was the medieval way of looking at the story. Castagno obviously thought otherwise: to him, David was an athletic young man whose courage came from God but whose strength and skill were his own. He wanted to show his hero in a fighting pose, and this is why he turned to Classical

54

sculpture for help, since the Ancients had known a great deal more about the human body in action than he did. The statue in figure 39 will show you how Castagno has followed the outlines of his Ancient model even to the wind-blown drapery. Curiously enough, however, the Classical warrior is not a heroic figure at all; in fact, he is running away and his hand is raised for protection. Castagno has changed the meaning of the pose from fear to defiance.

Castagno's David seems much less solid and bulky than the figures of Masaccio or Piero della Francesca. His forms are more graceful, tense, and nervous. We find a similar style in our next picture (figure 41), a dramatic Crucifixion panel by Andrea Mantegna, who was one of the first, and also the greatest, of the Early Renaissance masters in North Italy. He came from the town of Padua, near Venice, and it is likely that he was influenced by Castagno, who had done some murals in Venice during Mantegna's youth. His figures look even more strained than the *David*; the tautly stretched Christ and the mourning group under the cross to the left, are so intensely expressive that they make us think of Roger van der Weyden and *The Avignon Pietà*, while the deep, airy background landscape reminds us of the van Eyck *Crucifixion* in figure 29. As a North Italian, Mantegna understood Late Gothic painting better than the Florentine masters did, but he was also a keen student of scientific perspective. Instead of letting us float above the scene, the way the van Eycks had done, he gives us a front-row seat, as it were, on a level with the figures in the picture, so that we are far more directly involved with the tragic story before our eyes.

The difference between Late Gothic and Early Renaissance shows up particularly well

43. Piero di Cosimo. THE DISCOVERY OF HONEY. About 1498. Worcester Art Museum, Massachusetts

in the field of portrait painting. We are not sure who did the elegant young lady in figure 42—an important Florentine master, certainly, of the time around 1460—nor do we know her name, but she must have been one of the famous beauties of her day, and the picture is quite frankly meant to make us admire her beauty. One might almost call her a very refined pin-up girl, who knows her own good looks and is proud of them. Our artist has given her such a self-assured air that the *Young Princess* of the Master of Moulins (figure 33) seems downright timid by comparison.

In the color plate facing the title page of our book you see another kind of portrait. This picture of an old man and his grandson was probably ordered by the little boy's father, and for much the same reason that we today take family snapshots—to remind us of people we love. Domenico Ghirlandaio, who painted it in Florence about 1480, admired the realistic style of the Flemish masters. He has recorded the wrinkles, the warts, the diseased nose of the old man exactly as he saw them. But there is also something here that we don't find in Late Gothic portraits: the picture tells us not only what the old man looked like but what kind of a person he was. We would never think of comparing this face to a landscape (as we did with *The Man in the Red Turban* by Jan van Eyck in figure 30), because it is alive with the glow of love and tenderness. And the little boy looks up to his grandfather so trustingly that we, too, no longer mind the ugly, swollen nose and think only of the warm human feeling that links these two people.

The last two pictures in this chapter bring us back once more to the idea of the "rebirth of antiquity," since the subjects of both of them are taken from the religion of the Greeks and Romans. Needless to say, the Church frowned on such pagan stories, and yet we find more and more of them towards the end of the fifteenth century. Did the artists who painted them, and the patrons who owned them, actually believe in the Ancient gods? Certainly not. Sandro Botticelli, for instance, who did the famous *Birth of Venus* in figure 44, was a deeply religious man; neither he nor anybody else in Florence accepted the goddess of love as "real" the way they accepted Christ or the Madonna. If we want to understand this picture, we must think of it as a sort of poetic dream where Venus, born of the sea like a shimmering pearl, stands for that "rebirth of mankind" which was the great hope of the Renaissance. And she looks as frail as a dream, too—pale, delicate, without weight or bulk, she bends like a reed in the gentle breeze from the mouths of the two wind gods on the left. How solid and powerful the David of Castagno seems as against these gossamer creatures!

Our other "pagan" picture (figure 43), painted by Piero di Cosimo shortly before 1500, is the very opposite of Botticelli's *Venus*: down-to-earth, gay, and colorful. Here we see Bacchus, the god of wine, and his goat-footed companions, the satyrs, participating in a sort of revel on a sunny summer afternoon. The god himself, looking slightly tipsy, stands on the right with his lady-love, Ariadne, but most of the satyrs pay little attention to him; instead, they busy themselves about the old willow tree in the center of the scene. If you look closely,

56

44. Sandro Botticelli. THE BIRTH OF VENUS. About 1480–1485. Uffizi Gallery, Florence

you will find that they are all making as much noise as they can by banging their pots and pans, for they have discovered a swarm of bees, and the noise will make the bees settle in a cluster on one of the branches of the tree. The satyrs will then put them in a hive and, later on, collect the honey, from which they will make a kind of wine. Piero di Cosimo tells us all this in a high good humor, as if Bacchus and the satyrs were just plain, friendly country folk. And that, in a way, is what he really believed. The stories about the ancient gods, he thought, were actually about people who had lived in the early days of mankind, before history began. The discovery of honey must have been very important to these simple people; it was, after all, a first step towards civilization. That is why they honored the memory of the first bee-keepers by making gods out of them. Thus Bacchus and his companions in our picture stand for "man's slow progress through the ages"—a less poetic idea than Botticelli's dream of "mankind reborn," but a far more realistic one. Piero's style, too, is more realistic. Like Ghirlandaio, he was interested in Flemish painting; the fine airy landscape background of his picture shows this Northern influence particularly well. But the landscape is not merely pleasant to look at, it also helps to drive home the "lesson" of the story. The rough, barren hill on the right stands for the primitive early days of man's life on earth, while the one on the left, with its little town and steeple, tells us of the blessings of civilized living. Thus the entire panel reflects the hopeful outlook of the Early Renaissance.

57

THE AGE OF GENIUS

AS WE ENTER THE SIXTEENTH CENTURY, we almost come to feel that the idea of "rebirth" was more than an idle dream. There were so many great men that they seemed like a new race of giants, gifted with creative powers such as the human mind had never known before. At first glance, this Age of Genius may strike us as a much happier era than our own troubled times. In actual fact, however, it would be hard to find a century more unstable, more difficult to live in, than the sixteenth. It was a time of never-ending conflicts, both of arms and of ideas, for the discoveries of the previous hundred years had by now thoroughly upset the old order of things everywhere. The wealth of America and of other new-found lands across the ocean started a scramble for power among the nations of Western Europe, with colonies and overseas trade as the stakes. These wars, in turn, were all mixed up with the great religious crisis, which disturbed people more than anything else that happened during those trying days. Christianity was divided against itself and, for the first time, the Catholic Church met with opposition; in the countries north of the Alps, great reformers such as Martin Luther and John Calvin declared themselves independent of the authority of the Pope and established Protestant Churches of their own. The fact that they found so many followers shows that there was a need for this Reformation of faith, since the Catholic Church at that time was still bound by medieval ideas; but the struggle between the two opposing camps was so cruel and bloody that it made quite a few people lose their trust in religion altogether.

How, you may wonder, could great masterpieces of art be created in the midst of all this turmoil? It is indeed difficult to say why we find so many men of genius in some periods, and few or none in others. Still, let us keep in mind that the sixteenth century was also an age of challenge, when old barriers were breaking

45. Leonardo da Vinci. SKETCHES FOR THE BATTLE OF ANGHIARI. About 1504. Windsor Castle. Reproduced by Gracious Permission of H. M. the Queen

46. Leonardo da Vinci. MONA LISA. About 1505. Louvre Museum, Paris

down and vast new horizons were opening up everywhere. Perhaps this unsettled state of affairs gave men a better chance to stretch their minds, and to accomplish great things, than they could have found in a stable and orderly world.

THE HIGH RENAISSANCE IN ITALY

AMONG THE ARTISTS of this time, three are so famous that their names have become household words: Leonardo da Vinci, Michelangelo, and Raphael. They lived during the High Renaissance in Italy, a glorious period at the beginning of the century that was like the Classical Age of Ancient Greece. Leonardo da Vinci came closer to being an all-around genius than any other man in history, even though he proudly thought of himself first and foremost as an artist. But if we look into his notebooks and drawings, we find that his idea of art takes in a lot of things that we would call natural science today. He believed so strongly in the eye as the perfect instrument for exploring the natural world that to see and to know meant the same to him. Artists, he said, are the best scientists; not only do they observe things better than other people—they think about what they see, and then tell the rest of us about it in pictures. Nowadays scientists prefer to put their knowledge into words (they have had to invent a whole lot of new ones for this purpose), but in the Renaissance a good picture was still "worth a thousand words."

Leonardo's own drawings are so clear and full of life that even if we find it very difficult to decipher his notes (which are written backwards), we can grasp his ideas by just looking at the drawings he made to illustrate them. No matter what we may be particularly interested in, we are apt to find that Leonardo was interested in it, too. He was the first man to seriously investigate aerodynamics and to design flying machines; he also drew meticulous and wonderfully exact pictures of the interior anatomy of the human body. These were but a few facets of his scientific inquiries, and in all these fields, Leonardo was far ahead of his time. His scientific

47. Michelangelo. THE CREATION OF ADAM. From the Sistine Ceiling. 1508–1512. Vatican, Rome

HIEREMIAS

48. Michelangelo. THE PROPHET JEREMIAH. From the Sistine Ceiling. 1508–1512. Vatican, Rome

49. Raphael. THE EXPULSION OF HELIODORUS. 1512–1514. Vatican Palace, Rome

mind can also be seen at work in one of the many preparatory studies he drew for a big battle picture about 1504 (figure 45). The point of the drawing is that animals and men have the same sort of expression on their faces when they are moved by the same strong feeling. In this case it is rage, and the man, the lion, and the horses are all baring their teeth and snarling. Here we really have one of the earliest studies in psychology, the science of the mind, which we like to think is something very modern.

Leonardo never actually finished the battle scene, but during those same years he did his most famous painting, the *Mona Lisa* (figure 46). If you compare it with earlier Florentine portraits (figure 42 and frontispiece), you will see right away that Leonardo's seems more complete, more rounded. The figure, the low wall behind her, and the distant landscape are no longer set off against each other as separate things; the picture as a whole has become more important than any of its parts. This new harmony was one of the aims of the High Renaissance. Leonardo has achieved it here not only by composing the picture more carefully but by painting it as if everything were seen through a slight haze that swallows up the small details, softens the outlines, and blends the shapes and colors together. In this way he leaves a good deal to our imagination, and that is why the *Mona Lisa* strikes us as so wonderfully alive. This is true both of the landscape (where Leonardo suggests to us how the earth "grew" from rocks and water) and of the face, with its mysterious smile. What is the Mona Lisa

62

50. Raphael. MADONNA WITH THE INFANT CHRIST AND THE INFANT SAINT JOHN. 1507. Louvre Museum, Paris

51. Giorgione. THE CONCERT. About 1510. Louvre Museum, Paris

thinking about? That really depends on what we are thinking about as we look at her. Perhaps Leonardo himself was something like that; people always found him even-tempered and friendly, but nobody ever knew what was on his mind.

Michelangelo was in many ways the exact opposite of Leonardo. We know, in fact, that the two did not get on together at all. He, too, had many different strings to his bow—he was a sculptor, architect, and poet, as well as a painter—but he took no interest in science. Leonardo could compare a man's face with that of a lion or a horse because human beings

64

to him were simply part of nature as a whole. For Michelangelo, on the contrary, man was a unique and almost god-like thing; and the artist was not a calmly observing scientist but a creator under whose hands dead materials suddenly came to life. In order to do this, the artist needed more than a brilliant mind—he had to be inspired, and inspiration could come only from God, since the artist was, in a way, competing with Him. Michelangelo himself never knew whether to regard his gift as a blessing or a curse. His violent personality, always torn between hope and despair, filled those who knew him with such awe that they really felt there was something superhuman about him. He has done more than any other man to shape our idea of what genius is like, so that even now we still tend to think of it as a strange power that holds the artist in its grip.

Michelangelo's masterpiece is the huge fresco covering the entire ceiling of the Sistine Chapel in the Vatican. He did it between 1508 and 1512 for Julius II, the great Pope during whose reign Rome became the center of Italian art. Figure 47 shows you one of the main scenes, *The Creation of Adam*. It will remind you of the monumental style of Giotto and Masaccio, but there is a forcefulness of action and feeling here such as we have never seen before. These mighty creatures, stronger and more perfectly formed than any man could hope to be, come to us not from the *real* world of nature but from the *ideal* world of Michelangelo's imagination. The figure of God rushing through the sky is nothing less than creative energy itself. Adam, in contrast, still clings to the earth from which he has been molded. Their hands reach out to each other across space, and we can almost feel the breath of life flowing into Adam. No other artist has ever equaled Michelangelo's vision of this fateful moment. Around the main scenes on the ceiling there is a framework painted to look like stone, with seated figures in niches. One of these, the Prophet Jeremiah, is shown in figure 48. His body gives an even greater feeling of bulk and strength than those in *The Creation of Adam*, yet it is apparent that all his energy is turned inward upon the dark thoughts that fill his mind. This quality is made even more immediate when we realize that Michelangelo has portrayed something of his own character in this gloomy figure.

How different are the paintings of Raphael! Younger than Leonardo and Michelangelo, he was the happiest and least complicated of the three. He, too, came to Rome at the request of Julius II, but he had already seen Leonardo's work in Florence and learned a great deal from it. In the lovely Madonna panel of 1507 (figure 50), the softness of the modeling, the calm beauty of the Virgin, and the way her left arm is placed, show the influence of the *Mona Lisa*. Yet Raphael's works embody none of those disquieting mysteries that make Leonardo so difficult to understand.

In Rome, the Sistine Ceiling made a deep impression on Raphael. This phase of his style

65

52. Titian. THE ENTOMBMENT OF CHRIST. About 1525. Louvre Museum, Paris

may be seen in *The Expulsion of Heliodorus* (figure 49), one of the frescoes he painted in the Vatican Palace between 1512 and 1514. It illustrates the story of a pagan Greek soldier who had brashly entered the Temple in Jerusalem in order to carry off its treasures. In the center of the picture, the High Priest at the altar is asking the Lord's help, and his prayer brings the three armed messengers of God, on the right, who are chasing Heliodorus and his men away. These figures are as powerfully built as those in the Sistine Ceiling, and even more agitated. But with Raphael all the drama is turned into action, so there is no "battle of feelings" within these figures, such as we found in Michelangelo's style. What we admire most about *The Expulsion of Heliodorus*, however, is its masterly composition. Only a genius could have made a stable, well-balanced whole out of so many figures doing different things. The way they are fitted into the architectural framework, which forms the backbone of the entire picture, reminds us of Masaccio's *Trinity* mural (figure 35), except that Raphael's design is far richer and full of movement.

After the death of Julius II in 1513, Rome did not long remain the great center of art it had been. Meanwhile, a new school of painting had grown up in the rich seafaring and trading city of Venice, in the northeast corner of Italy. The first master of the Venetian High Renaissance was Giorgione, who died in 1510 when he was still in his early twenties. We know only about a half dozen pictures that can be attributed to him, yet he is ranked among the greatest painters in history, for it was he who brought to Venetian painting most of the special qualities that set it apart from all the other styles of the sixteenth century.

53. Titian. MAN IN A RED CAP. About 1530. The Frick Collection, New York

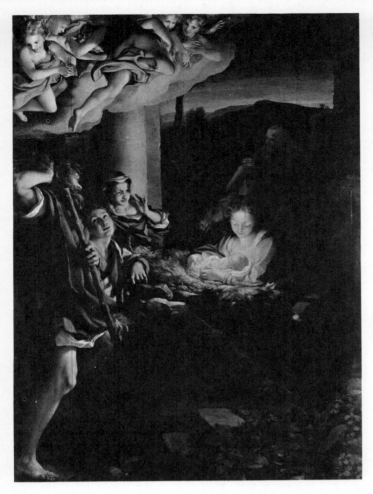

54. Correggio. THE HOLY NIGHT. About 1530. Gallery, Dresden

In his splendid *Concert* (figure 51), we find it hard to tell what kind of story the artist had in mind. The more we look at the figures, the less certain we become about what exactly they are doing. All we can say is that they seem happy in each other's company. Perhaps the difference between the two young men gives us a clue to the riddle: one is a barefoot boy, very simply dressed, while the lute-player sports an elegant and colorful costume. Could Giorgione have wanted to contrast country life and city life in these figures? As for the two women, we know only that they must have a Classical meaning of some sort; they are probably nymphs or similar woodland spirits in human shape as imagined by the Ancients.

Oddly enough, however, not knowing the story seems to make little difference to us. The charm of the picture, we feel, is in its mood rather than its action, as if the artist had made up a poem—calm and gentle, yet a little sad, too—and then painted it instead of writing it down. Now, Giorgione was not the first painter to be interested in mood, but with him it became more important than anything else. Michelangelo and Raphael had created an ideal world through their mastery of form; Giorgione created *his* ideal world—a warmer and more human one than theirs—out of light and color. Instead of making us stand in awe, he invites us inside to share it with him. In the *Concert*, the golden rays of a setting sun bring all the details into harmony. If we could only make this wonderful moment last forever! But the shadows are deepening, and night will be here soon.

68

55. Veronese. CHRIST IN THE HOUSE OF LEVI. 1573. Academy, Venice

Giorgione's new way of painting was explored further by Titian, who outlived him by a great many years and who was to become the most brilliant and famous of all Venetian artists. Titian, however, also knew something of the work of Michelangelo and Raphael. In the *Entombment of Christ* (figure 52), which he did about 1525, the figures are far more powerfully built and more expressive than those of Giorgione, and the design is more monumental. Even so, we are again touched more deeply by the mood of the scene than by the action; and this mood depends on the kind of lighting and color we saw in the *Concert*. The darkening sky, the rapidly fading sunlight make the grief of the mourners seem particularly real—they cannot bear the thought of leaving the dead Savior, and yet they must place him in the grave before evening turns into night. So the men force themselves to finish their task while the women take a last look at the limp, pitiful body.

Titian's greatest fame was as a painter of portraits. All the important men of his day, from the Pope and Emperor on down, were eager to have their pictures done by him. You will understand why if you look at the *Man in a Red Cap* (figure 53), which shows all his mastery of light and color. With quick, feathery strokes of the brush, Titian captures the "feel" of the materials so completely that they seem richer and more precious to us than they would be in real life. And the unknown sitter, too, we suspect, looks more attractive than he actually was—not more beautiful, perhaps, but more interesting, more sensitive. Lost in

69

56. Grünewald. ANNUNCIATION, MADONNA WITH ANGELS, RESURRECTION.

his own thoughts, the young man seems quite unaware of us. It is this slight touch of sadness that gives him such unusual appeal in our eyes.

The new broad manner of using oil paint introduced by Giorgione and Titian no longer demanded the smooth surface of wooden panels. The Venetian masters preferred to do their pictures on heavy canvas cloth. This was found to be so much cheaper and more convenient that painters have been using canvas ever since. It also allowed the Venetians to make

70

oil paintings as large as wall paintings. *Christ in the House of Levi* (figure 55), done in 1573 by Paolo Veronese, is a splendid example of such a wall decoration. The sparkling, colorful costumes and the splendid architecture make us think of an exuberant party in the palace of some Venetian lord, rather than of a story from the Bible. But if the picture does not strike a very religious mood, Veronese gives us a wonderfully rich and vivid account of the festive scene, as if he had staged this pageant of Venetian life for our special benefit.

57. Dürer. Self-Portrait.
1484. Albertina, Vienna

58. Dürer. Self-Portrait.
1500. Pinakothek, Munich

59. Dürer. Demonstration of Perspective.
Woodcut, 1525

The cities of Florence, Rome, and Venice were the main centers of Italian art during the sixteenth century. But we also find some important painters in smaller cities. The most original of these was Correggio, who came from a small town near Parma. In his *Holy Night* (figure 54), done about 1530, the bold lighting looks very Venetian, while the figures show that he must have known something of Leonardo, Michelangelo, and Raphael. And yet the picture as a whole is quite unlike any of theirs. First of all, the figures don't stay put inside the frame but keep bursting into the picture from outside, like the huge shepherd on the left or the whirling cloud of angels above him. Obviously, Correggio is much less interested in balanced design than he is in making us feel the excitement of the story. He shows us the birth of Christ as a great miracle, but one that looks real and natural, too. That is why he has made it a night scene lit up by the new-born Child, just as Gentile da Fabriano had done (compare figure 27). In his own day Correggio was not regarded very highly. But a century later many other painters took over his sensational style, and he suddenly became as famous as the great masters of Rome and Venice.

THE NORTHERN RENAISSANCE

AROUND 1500 the painters of Northern Europe showed a growing interest in Italian art. The Late Gothic style, however, was still very much alive, and there followed a long tug-of-war between the two until the Italian influence finally won out. We can get a good idea of this "battle of styles" by comparing the two greatest Northern painters of that time, Matthias Grünewald and Albrecht Dürer. Both of these men were Germans whose backgrounds had much in common; and yet their aims were as different as could be. Grünewald's masterpiece, *The Isenheim Altar*, was done at just about the same time that Michelangelo finished the Sistine Ceiling. Its four huge wooden wings are painted on both sides (figure 56 shows you the altar with the outer panels opened up). Grünewald had already felt the influence of Renaissance art: he knew more about perspective than he could have learned from the Late Gothic alone, and some of his figures, too, are surprisingly solid and vigorous. But his imagination is still completely Late Gothic, and he uses Italian ideas only in order to make this world of dreams and visions more real, more exciting than ever before. *The Isenheim Altar* is the final outburst of this particular kind of creative energy—an energy so intense that everything in these panels twists and turns as though it had a life of its own. Let us compare the *Annunciation* on the left-hand wing, for instance, with the earlier panel by Roger van der Weyden (figure 31). Roger's Christ enters so quietly that he hardly seems to move at all, while Grünewald's angel is blown into the room by a tremendous gust of air that makes the Virgin reel backwards. On the two center panels a fairy-tale orchestra of angels entertains the Madonna and the new-born Child. There is a great burst of light above the clouds from which God the Father, in all His glory, gazes upon the young mother and her babe. In this tender and poetic vision, Heaven and earth have truly become one in celebrating the miracle of Christ's birth. Among all the pictures we have seen so far, only the *Holy Night* of Correggio arouses similar feelings, different as it is in every other way.

The *Resurrection*, on the right, is the most dramatic panel of *The Isenheim Altar*. Here an even more awesome miracle happens before our eyes: Christ leaves the earth and becomes

60. Dürer. Knight, Death, and the Devil. Engraving, 1513

God once more. But he does not merely *rise* from the grave—he *explodes* upward in a spiraling rush, still trailing his shroud and shining with a light as brilliant as the sun against the midnight sky, while the guardians of the tomb, the forces of death, blindly grope along the ground in utter defeat. Here the strange genius of Grünewald has created its most unforgettable image.

Little is known about Grünewald's life. In the case of Dürer, on the other hand, we can trace his development almost year by year. Figure 57 shows you a drawing he made of himself in 1484, when he was only thirteen and had just started his training under a painter in his home town of Nuremberg.

73

Even then, Dürer could draw with great delicacy and assurance, but the style of the portrait is still entirely Late Gothic. Its sensitive, yet curiously timid look will remind you of the *Young Princess* by the Master of Moulins (figure 33). If we now turn to the painted self-portrait (figure 58) done in the year 1500, we can't help wondering whether this impressive, almost Christ-like figure is really the same person as the unsure boy of the drawing. During those sixteen years, everything about Dürer had changed: his style, his ideas, and his way of looking at himself. On his first visit to Italy, Dürer discovered both a new kind of art and a new kind of artist. He had been brought up to think of painters as modest craftsmen; in the South, he found, they were learned men who enjoyed the same respect as scientists, scholars, and philosophers. So he decided not only to make the Italian style his own, but to educate himself in all the fields of learning that went with this new approach to art. More than that, he felt called upon to spread his own knowledge among his fellow artists, like a missionary preaching a new faith. In the self-portrait of 1500, he sees himself in this important new role; it is an idealized picture of the artist, much as the *Mona Lisa* is an idealized portrait of a woman.

Dürer's "mission" was helped a great deal by the fact that he was the finest print-maker of his time. These prints were of two kinds: engravings, where the lines of the picture are cut into a sheet of copper with a steel point; and woodcuts, where the spaces between the lines are carved out of the surface of a wooden block, leaving a raised design. Both copper plates and woodblocks can then be inked and many copies can be printed. Such prints, needless to say, are much cheaper than paintings, so that a great many more people can afford to buy them. The woodcut in figure 59 is from a book Dürer wrote about scientific perspective (this was another idea he got from Italy—you will recall that Piero della Francesca had written a similar book). It shows a contraption for making correctly foreshortened pictures in a purely mechanical, scientific way. The two men are "drawing" the lute on the table as it would appear to us if we looked at it from the spot on the right-hand wall where you see a little hook with a string passing through it. Dürer knew, of course, that such pictures were not works of art but simply records of a scientific experiment. He just wanted to prove that "correct" perspective did not depend on anybody's skill or judgment. Still, devices like this led people to invent better ways of making mechanical pictures. Soon the hook-and-string was replaced by the *camera obscura*, a box with a lens at one end and a screen of oiled paper at the other. The image projected by the lens could then be traced directly on paper, or, as in the camera of today, recorded on film.

But Dürer did not imitate Italian art slavishly. He picked what he thought interesting and impressive and then combined it with his own ideas, in the spirit of his own time and place. In his splendid engraving of 1513, *Knight, Death, and the Devil* (figure 60), the horse and rider have the calmness, the solid and monumental form of similar Italian works, such as the mounted soldiers of Piero della Francesca (figure 37), while Death and the Devil show the

74

61. Hans Holbein the Younger. GEORGE GISZE. 1532. State Museums, Berlin

same weird imagination that we know from the Van Eyck *Last Judgment* (figure 29). The contrast between the two styles helps to make Dürer's idea clear: his Knight is the exact opposite of those idle pleasure-seekers in Jerome Bosch's *Ship of Fools* (figure 34). He "knows where he is going"; his journey through life follows the road to Heaven (represented by the city in the distance) no matter how frightful the dangers along the way. The words of the famous hymn, "Onward, Christian Solidiers," might well serve as a title for Dürer's picture.

Hans Holbein the Younger was the last of the great German masters of this period. His best known works are the portraits he did in England, where he spent the later years of his life as court painter to King Henry VIII. The portrait of George Gisze (figure 61), painted in 1532, strikes a happy balance between the Northern European love of fine surface detail and the solidity and dignity of Italian Renaissance art. While the sitter has not been idealized in any way, his pose has something of the restful, harmonious quality of the *Mona Lisa*; and compared to Late Gothic portraits, this young merchant seems to have a new confidence in himself and in his own worth. It is perhaps for this reason that he commissioned the artist to portray him. Holbein shows him in his office, surrounded by business papers, seals, writing equipment, even a vase of flowers. These things only add to the feeling of quiet pride conveyed by the picture as a whole.

At the time Holbein came to England, the religious Reformation movement was already widespread in Northern Europe, and artists felt its effect more directly, perhaps, than anyone else. The new forms of faith all agreed on one point: religious art, they claimed, tempted people to worship statues and pictures rather than God himself. Wherever the Reformers won, the Church no longer demanded—and in some countries it even prohibited—the sacred sub-

jects that had been the mainstay of medieval art. As a result, religious pictures became much less important than before, since painters had to turn to other subjects in order to make a living. Holbein, as we have seen, concentrated on portraits. In figure 62 you meet a different kind of new subject. The picture was painted in 1567 by the great Flemish master Pieter Bruegel, at a time when the Netherlands, under th banner of the Reformation, were fighting a bloody war of independence against Catholic Spain. It shows the *Land of Cockayne*, a kind of fool's paradise where tables are always laden with tasty dishes, houses with roofs made of pies, and other wonders. Bruegel, of course, wants to teach us a moral lesson, but he no longer needs religion for this. The men under the tree are not unhappy sinners in the grip of evil; they *could* act as responsible human beings but, like most people, they are not wise enough to know what is best for them in the long run. By becoming slaves to their appetites,

76

62. Bruegel. THE LAND OF COCKAYNE. 1567. Pinakothek, Munich

they have given up all ambition, all self-respect, for the sake of a kind of animal happiness:
the knight has dropped his lance, the farmer his flail, and the scholar, on the right, has given
up his books. "Beware of the fool's paradise," Bruegel seems to say, "it's more dangerous
than hell because people *like* going there."

MANNERISM

IN ITALY, the home of the Catholic Church, the Reformation did not touch the artists
directly. Yet there, too, the great crisis of faith had a deeply unsettling effect upon
their work. After 1520, the confidence of the High Renaissance in the almost divine powers
of the human spirit was no longer shared by the younger artists; to them, man seemed once

77

63. Parmigianino. SELF-PORTRAIT. 1524. Kunsthistorisches Museum, Vienna

again at the mercy of forces over which he had no control. So they began to show the human figure in strange new ways, twisting it into ever more impossible poses and pulling it out to unnatural height. Some of them even developed a strong taste for the Late Gothic. This disturbing phase of Italian art used to be looked down upon as the "decay of the Renaissance"; that is what the label "Mannerism" meant. But we now accept it as an important style in its own right, and the highly personal flavor of the best of the Mannerists seems particularly exciting to modern eyes—perhaps because we, too, no longer believe in fixed ideals in art. You can see the beginning of the new style in the extraordinary *Self-Portrait* (figure 63) done in 1524 by a young painter from Parma called Parmigianino. It shows the artist exactly as he saw himself in one of those round, convexly curved distorting mirrors, so that his hand looks monstrously large and the walls and ceiling of the room are bent into curves. Why was Parmigianino so fascinated by these distorted shapes? Was it merely scientific curiosity, or had he come to feel that there was no such thing as a steady, "correct" reality, that everything depended on what your personal point of view might happen to be?

In Parmigianino's picture the artist still faces the outside world, even if he does it "through the looking glass." The early Mannerists working in Florence went even further; they depended far less on nature than on their own private worlds of dreams and visions. This is certainly true of the superbly dramatic *Descent from the Cross* in figure 65, which was done in 1521 by a painter known simply as Rosso (or, sometimes, Rosso Fiorentino). The spidery, angular figures, their frenzied gestures and expressions, the weird, unreal light—all these give the picture a ghostly, frightening quality that is not soon

78

64. Tintoretto. PRESENTATION OF THE VIRGIN. About 1550. Church of Santa Maria dell'Orto, Venice

forgotten. Rosso's men and women are no longer acting, they are being acted upon; their garments, and their very bodies, have turned brittle, as though frozen by a sudden blast of cold. Nothing could be more remote from the Classical balance of the High Renaissance than this nightmarish, "anti-Classical" style.

65. Rosso. Descent from the Cross. 1521. Volterra

In Venice, Mannerism did not appear so quickly, but by the middle of the century we find it firmly established in the work of Tintoretto, who was certainly the most important Venetian master after Titian. His *Presentation of the Virgin* (figure 64), is less "anti-Classical" than Rosso's *Descent*; the vigorous poses of some of the figures may remind you of Michelangelo, whom Tintoretto admired greatly. Even so, you can feel the Mannerist spirit in the odd perspective, in the strange, unsteady light with its sudden bright flashes and deep, inky shadows, and in the over-dramatic gestures of the figures as they watch the twelve-year-old Mary going up the steps to the Temple. What matters most to Tintoretto is not the simple, straightforward story from the life of the Virgin but the tense, excited air he has given to the scene, as if we were witnessing some tremendous drama.

This style of painting fitted in well with a new trend in the Catholic world. In defense against the Reformation, the Church had begun to place more stress on the mystical and supernatural parts of religious experience. This "Counter-Reformation" was strongest in Spain, and in Spain, too, we find the last and most striking of the Mannerist painters. He is known today simply as El Greco, "the Greek," since he came from the island of Crete. His style of painting, however, was formed in Venice, under the influence of Tintoretto and other masters. He went to Spain as a mature artist and settled in the town of Toledo. El Greco's first great success there was the *Assumption* (figure 66), of 1577. It shows the Virgin Mary being carried to Heaven after her death, in the presence of the Apostles. The sudden flashes of light and the curiously unreal colors will remind you of Tintoretto, but in spirit the work seems closer to Rosso's *Descent*. Here again we find the sharp-edged, "frozen" draperies, the angular, frantic gestures, the drawn-out limbs. And El Greco handles space in an even more personal way than Rosso; he uses foreshortening, but without perspective, so that we cannot tell from what level we are viewing the scene. Then, too, there is a good deal of modeling in every figure, and yet they look like cardboard cutouts placed one over the other, with no space between them. Thus El Greco makes it quite impossible for us to separate the real from the unreal, the world of feeling from the world we can see and touch.

66. El Greco. Assumption of the Virgin. 1577. The Art Institute of Chicago

THE TRIUMPH OF LIGHT

IT IS NOT EASY to define the spirit of seventeenth-century art. We often speak of it as the Baroque, but nobody seems to be quite sure what this means, or ought to mean. The word itself might be compared to the term Gothic, which at one time merely indicated that the art of the late Middle Ages was clumsy and of poor quality, although it has become thoroughly respectable since then. Baroque, too, started out as an insulting tag for certain kinds of seventeenth-century art, but because it did not come into general use until recent times, its negative meaning has not yet worn off completely (there are still many who consider Baroque as a synonym for "excessive"). Quite a few people still feel that it is all right to call *some* seventeenth-century artists Baroque but not others. In this book we shall be less cautious; we shall use Baroque for the last phase of the Renaissance era (after Early Renaissance, High Renaissance, and Mannerism), just as Gothic means the last phase of the Middle

82   67. Caravaggio. THE CARDSHARPS. About 1590. Private Collection

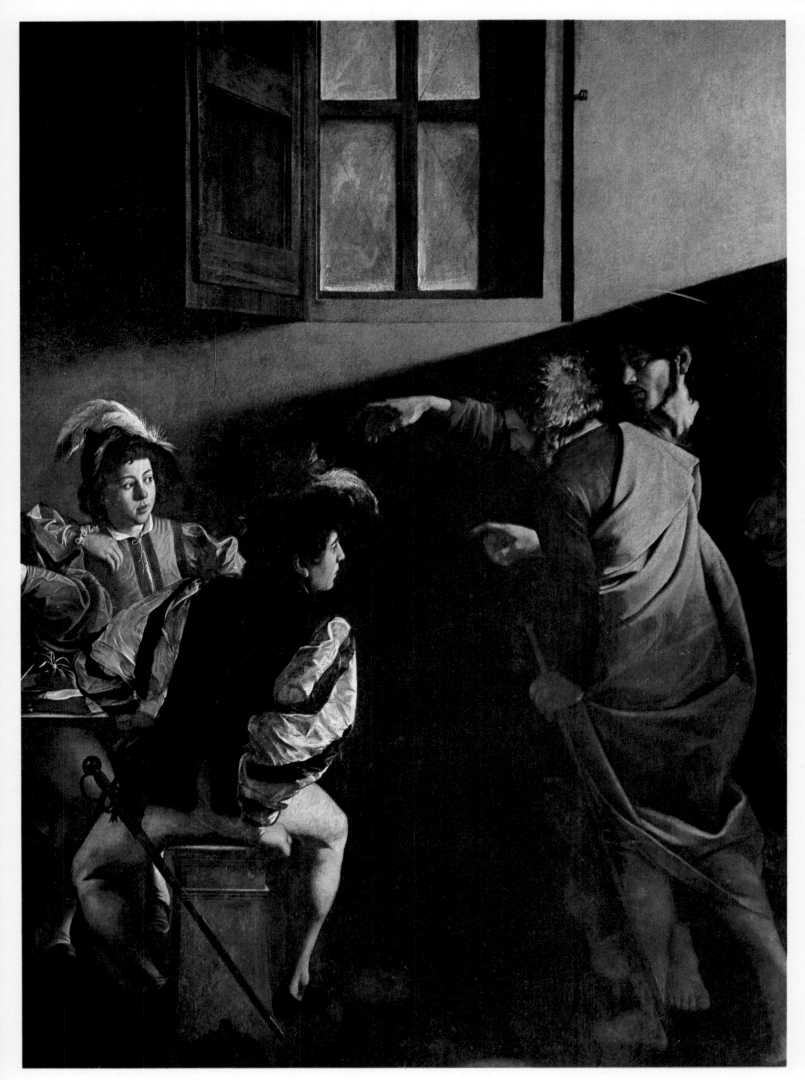

68. Caravaggio. THE CALLING OF SAINT MATTHEW (detail). 1597–98. Church of San Luigi dei Francesi, Rome

69. Rubens. Crucifixion Altar. 1620. Museum, Antwerp

Ages. If you think of it like that you will understand more easily how seventeenth-century art could be as rich and varied as it was and yet have a decided character of its own.

In many ways the Baroque Age is a summing up of all the different trends we have seen since the early fifteenth century. People were no longer so upset by the exciting new ideas and discoveries that had brought the medieval world to an end; they had learned how to live with them and what to do with them. Earlier, we had found daring explorers like Columbus setting out to bring back the riches of unknown lands. These were now followed by colonists, such as the Pilgrim Fathers who settled in New England in 1620. The countries along the Atlantic coast of Europe—England, Holland, France, and Spain—had all gained important overseas territories and grew more prosperous and powerful than they had been before, while Germany and Italy became less so. In the sciences, we no longer find all-around geniuses like Leonardo and Dürer opening up new fields of knowledge all at once. They had taught the specialists how to use their eyes, but it remained for the latter to describe the workings of nature in an orderly and systematic manner. So now there were men such as Galileo and Newton, who summed up the behavior of moving bodies in a few simple laws that held good for every kind of motion, whether of the earth circling around the sun or of an apple dropping from a tree. These important scientists of the Baroque Age laid the foundation for the technical marvels of our own day.

The struggle between the Reformation movement and the defenders of the old faith had reached a stalemate, with the ideologies of both factions attaining a type of stability, so that there was less open conflict than before. The Catholic Church, its strength revived by the Counter-Reformation, could feel secure once more, and the city of Rome again became the goal of artists from all over Europe. They came, of course, to study the great masterpieces of Classical Antiquity and of the High Renaissance; but they also learned from the Italian artists of their own time, and these, in turn, picked up ideas from them. In fact, seventeenth-century Rome was a sort of melting pot of styles, where North and South, past and present, flowed together in an endless and bewildering stream. Every visitor came away from it with different impressions, yet the experience gave all of them something in common—enough, at any rate, to make us feel that the Baroque was an international style, however much it might vary from one place to the next.

84

70. Rubens. MARIE DE'MEDICI, QUEEN OF FRANCE, LANDING IN MARSEILLES. Sketch. About 1622. Pinakothek, Munich

The foreign artists who arrived in Rome towards the year 1600 found the Italians all excited about a young painter named Caravaggio, who had himself come to the city only a few years before from a town in Northern Italy. A look at his *Cardsharps* (figure 67), done about 1590, will make you realize how little his work has in common with the strained, other-worldly art of the Mannerists. Caravaggio had learned a good deal from the Venetian High Renaissance style (compare figures 51 and 53), but he refused to idealize his figures. His own outlook was naturalistic, which means that he wanted to show the world just as he saw it in every day life. In our picture he has painted some soldiers such as one might have met in any Roman tavern, playing a crooked game of cards: the young scoundrel on the right has some extra cards hidden behind his back and is about to spring them on his victim, following a signal from the older man in the center. Will they get away with this, we wonder, or is there going to be a fight? Caravaggio does not tell us; he only builds up the suspense. Clearly, there is no moral lesson to be learned here. At first people were shocked at this kind of subject —they claimed it was neither noble nor beautiful enough for a large painting. Yet they couldn't help admiring the way Caravaggio had made the group come to life. Two things impressed them particularly: Caravaggio's new sense of timing, which let him catch his characters at exactly the right moment; and his dramatic use of light and dark. He was the first painter who spotlighted his pictures like a stage director, contrasting brilliant highlights with sharply outlined, deep shadows, in order to make every face, every gesture as expressive as possible. If the *Cardsharps* were bathed in a soft, gentle light, a great deal of the tense, gripping air that holds our attention and creates the mood would doubtless be lacking.

71. Terbrugghen. Lute Player. About 1620–25. National Museum, Stockholm

A few years later, in *The Calling of Saint Matthew* (figure 68 is a detail), Caravaggio took an even bolder step: he painted a story from the life of Christ as if it were happening right then and there in a Roman tavern. The men sitting at a table in this drab, dark basement room clearly belong to the same disreputable class of soldiers we know from the *Cardsharps*. The Saint, who sits with this group, does not appear in our color plate (the red sleeve on the extreme left is his). The Saviour appears on the right with one of his disciples. They are obviously poor and humble people—both of them are barefoot, and their simple dress makes a strong contrast with the colorful costumes of the others. As Christ raises his arm in a beckoning gesture, a golden beam of sunlight falls through the window behind him and carries

86

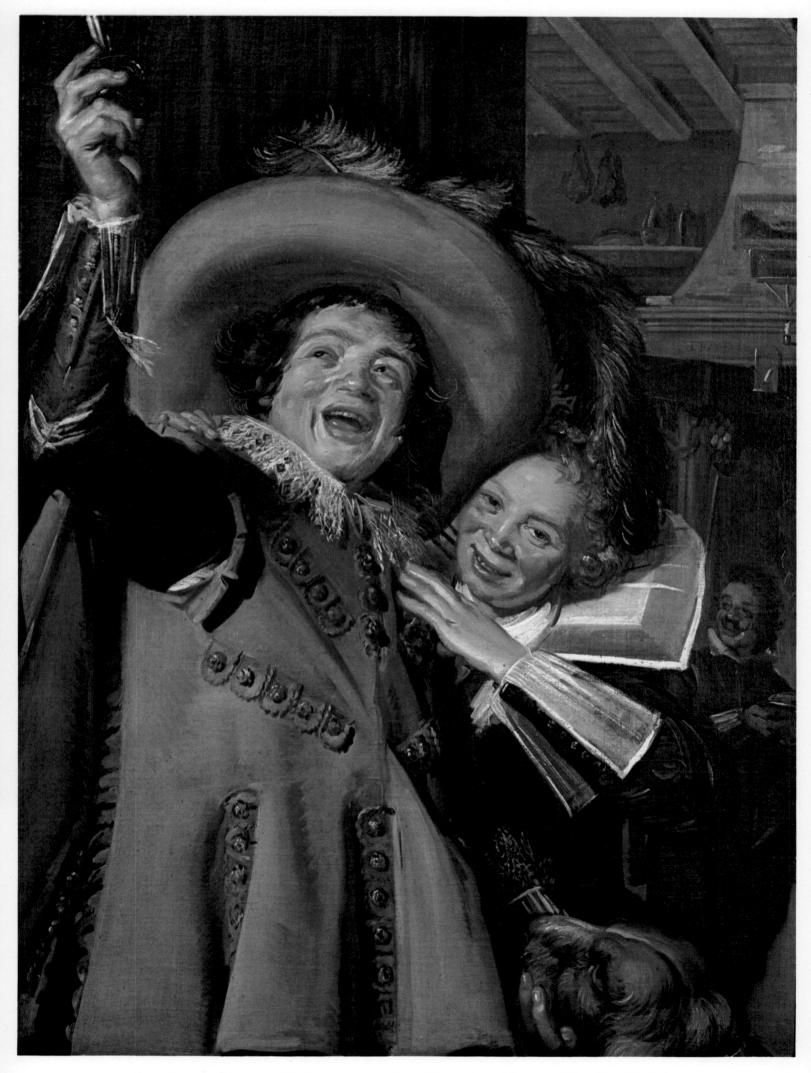

72. Hals. Yonker Ramp and His Sweetheart. 1623. Metropolitan Museum of Art, New York

73. Rembrandt. THE POLISH RIDER. About 1655. The Frick Collection, New York

his call across to Matthew. It seems a perfectly natural kind of light, but the way it points at Matthew and lets the hand and face of Christ suddenly emerge from the dark, gives it a symbolic meaning, too. As a matter of fact, this beam is by far the most important thing in the picture. Take it away, and all the magic, all the expressive power, disappears with it. You will understand now how Caravaggio could translate an important Biblical story such as this into the workaday reality of his own time and yet fill it with the deepest religious feeling; it is his discovery of light *as a force* that raises this tavern scene to the level of a sacred event.

Caravaggio's naturalism seemed less strange to visiting foreigners than it did to the Italians. But then, the human, everyday approach to religious stories had been familiar to Northern artists ever since Gothic times. While he was not exactly a prophet without honor in his own country, it was in the Netherlands, in France, and in Spain that Caravaggio left the deepest impression. His ideas influenced all the important masters of Baroque painting, even those who became far more famous than he did.

The first of these, Peter Paul Rubens, was from Flanders, the southern part of the Netherlands that had remained Catholic and under Spanish rule when Holland, the northern half, had managed to gain its independence. As a young man Rubens spent eight years in Italy, eagerly studying the works of the great painters from the High Renaissance to his own day. By the time he returned home to the city of Antwerp, he had learned very much more about Italian art than any Northern artist before him. It might well be said of him, in fact, that he finished what Dürer had started to do a hundred years earlier—to break down the barriers of taste and style between North and South. The wonderful *Crucifixion* of 1620 (figure 69) shows you how much Rubens owed to the Italians: here you find the powerful bodies of Michelangelo and Raphael, the sparkling color of Titian, the sweep of Correggio, the naturalism, the drama, and the spotlighting of Caravaggio, along with a force of expression that will remind you of

74. Rembrandt. CHRIST IN THE STORM ON THE LAKE OF GALILEE. 1633. Isabella Stewart Gardner Museum, Boston

75. Rembrandt. SAUL AND DAVID. About 1660. Mauritshuis Museum, The Hague

Grünewald. The amazing thing about Rubens' genius is not only that he was able to digest all these different sources, so very skillfully that we don't even know they are there unless we make a special point of looking for them. If he borrows the "words" of other artists, he gives them a new sound and a new meaning, so that they become part of his own personal "language." And what an exciting, colorful language it is! For Rubens, nothing ever stands still; all his forms are alive with a flowing, swirling movement that sweeps through the picture like a windstorm. A Rubens scene is never complete in itself—it spills over the edges of the canvas on every side, and the frame simply cuts across it (just compare his *Crucifixion* with the one by Mantegna in figure 41). The idea of composing pictures in this way came, of course, from Correggio, but Rubens carried it a great deal further. "After all," he seems to be telling us, "in the real world there are no limits to space or time; life as we know it means change, movement, action. Why should things be different in the world of art?"

You can see all this even better in our next picture (figure 70), which is a small sketch for

90

a very large painting, one of a series Rubens did in 1621-25 for the Queen of France. It shows her arrival in Marseilles (she was Italian and had come to France by boat). Not a very exciting story, you might say—but Rubens turns it into a glorious, swirling, exciting spectacle of a kind we have never seen before. As the Queen walks down the gangplank, the winged figure of Fame flying overhead sounds a blast on his trumpets, and Neptune, the mythological god of the sea, emerges from the deep with his fish-tailed crew; they have guarded the Queen's ship during her journey, and are overjoyed at her safe landing. In this festive scene everything flows together: heaven and earth, fantasy and reality, motion and emotion—even drawing and painting. For in our sketch these two have become the same thing. Rubens could not plan the design of the picture without thinking of light and color from the very start, just as in real life there are no forms apart from light and color. It is this unified way of seeing that makes his work, and Baroque art in general, so different from all earlier styles.

While Rubens became the most famous artist of his time in the Catholic half of Europe, the first great painters of the Protestant world appeared in Holland. As a wealthy nation of merchants and seafarers, proud of their hard-won freedom, the Dutch developed such an appetite for pictures of themselves and of their way of life that their artists had quite enough to do even without working for the Church. In fact, Holland probably had more painters, and more art collectors, than any other country during the seventeenth century. Pictures were as popular then as movies or sports are today, so that many Dutchmen were lured into becoming painters by hopes of success which all too often failed to come true. At times even the greatest artists of Holland found themselves suddenly out of favor with the public and hard-pressed for a living. Actually, this boom only lasted for about half a century, but these years are one of the most important chapters in the history of painting.

76. Van Goyen. FORT ON A RIVER. 1644. Museum of Fine Arts, Boston

77. Jacob van Ruisdael. THE JEWISH GRAVEYARD. About 1655. Picture Gallery, Dresden

Not many Dutch painters traveled to Italy. However, in the early years of the century we find several that did; they are known as the Utrecht School, after the name of their home town. In Rome, these men were so impressed with the style of Caravaggio that they looked at little else. The charming *Lute Player* (figure 71) by Hendrick Terbrugghen, the most talented member of this group, seems to come from the same tavern as Caravaggio's young soldiers; the naturalism, the light, the timing, all remind us of the *Cardsharps*. These were the things Terbrugghen and his friends brought home with them to Holland, for other painters to see and get excited about. In doing so, they became the connecting link between the art of Caravaggio and the great masters of their own country, who knew better than they did how to put the new Italian ideas to work.

That is what has happened in the wonderfully lively portrait of *Yonker Ramp and His Sweetheart* (figure 72), which was done in 1623 by Frans Hals, the leading painter of the town of Haarlem. It is hard to imagine, for instance, Titian's young nobleman (figure 53) or Holbein's successful and serious George Gisze (figure 61) wanting to be shown like this drinking and carousing with a lusty bar wench. Yet the young Dutch cavalier of our painting obviously did not mind posing as the main figure in an uninhibited (even undignified) tavern scene. Apparently he wanted liveliness rather than dignity, and Frans Hals has given him more of that than even Caravaggio could have done. Everything here is keyed to the mood of the moment: the laughter, the raising of the wine glass, and—most important of all—the way the picture is painted. Frans Hals has put down his colors in broad, dashing strokes of the brush, never really "finishing" any of the details, so that the completed picture keeps the freshness of a first sketch (compare the one by Rubens, figure 70). We can almost see the artist battling against time, making every split second count. How happy he would have been with a modern camera! Or so, at least, it seems to us; actually it must have taken Frans Hals hours, not minutes, to do a life-size painting such as this. What matters is that he wanted us to *think* he did it in the wink of an eye.

For many years Frans Hals was among the busiest and most prosperous portrait painters of Holland, but as he grew older the public turned away from him and he found himself "out of fashion." A similar fate fell to Rembrandt, the greatest genius of Dutch art. In figure 74 you see one of his earlier pictures, done in 1633, soon after he had settled in Amsterdam. For about a decade, it was the height of fashion for the wealthy people of this rich seaport city to have their portraits painted by Rembrandt. He himself, however, was more interested in his religious scenes, of which he did a great many, although for private collectors rather than for churches. The subject of ours is *Christ in the Storm on the Lake of Galilee*. Here Rembrandt shows how close he could come to Rubens: the forces of wind and water are clashing so fiercely that they almost seem to merge into one, crushing the boat between them. For the Dutch, who always felt the threat of the sea, either as sailors or as lowland dwellers, this scene had a very direct bearing on their daily lives; they could easily imagine themselves in the same boat with Christ, especially since Rembrandt has painted a fishing boat of the kind actually in use during those days. And the followers of Christ are just as scared as ordinary fishermen (one of them is even being seasick). But the most remarkable thing in the picture is the light, which reveals the entire scene to us in a single flash, as though it came from a terrific bolt of lightning. This is Caravaggio's dramatic timing again, put to work by Rembrandt and raised to a new pitch of excitement.

As Rembrandt grew older he became less and less interested in scenes of violent action. Instead, he gained a new insight into the drama of people's

78. Heda. STILL LIFE. 1634. Boymans Museum, Rotterdam

thoughts and feelings. *The Polish Rider* (figure 73) was done some twenty years after the *Christ in the Storm*, in this more personal style. We do not know for sure whether the rider is Polish (the title was given to him later), only that he is dressed in a strange, Eastern-looking costume. Nor can we tell exactly what meaning Rembrandt had in mind for him. Like Dürer, Rembrandt was a maker of prints, so he probably knew and admired the famous engraving, *Knight, Death, and the Devil* (figure 60). *The Polish Rider* is another "Christian Soldier," bravely riding through a perilous world; but here the dangers along the way, and the goal as well, are left to our imagination, instead of being spelled out as in Dürer's print. The gloomy landscape and somber colors suggest that our "knight" is not having an easy time; his serious, alert glance also tells us of unseen dangers, while the determined set of his mouth makes us feel that he will face them with courage.

If *Christ in the Storm* made us think of Rubens, *The Polish Rider* reminds us of Giorgione and Titian. Like them, Rembrandt has now become a poet of light and color, a maker of moods rather than of stories. And yet *The Polish Rider* remains a Baroque picture. Giorgione (figure 51) respects the limits of his canvas, he makes all his forms stay within the frame; with Rembrandt, on the contrary, the frame does not hold anything in place. His horseman is merely "passing through" and will soon be out of sight. And since he moves in the same direction as the light in the picture, we almost come to feel that the light is a kind of force which helps him along. The language of Rembrandt's late style, then, is not so different from that of Rubens after all; he just uses it to say other things.

The magic of light plays an even greater part in the religious works of Rembrandt's old age, such as the unforgettable *Saul and David* (figure 75). The Bible tells us that after his victory over Goliath, David was taken into the royal household, but that King Saul grew jealous when people praised the young hero more highly than him. One day, while David was playing the harp, he suddenly hurled his spear at the boy. Here is a subject ready-made for Rubens: what a splendid action picture he would have made of it! Rembrandt, on the other hand, shows us not the story itself but the meaning behind it. His Saul is not simply the victim of an evil passion, but a sad and lonely man so overcome with feeling that he forgets all about his royal dignity—he uses a curtain to wipe away his tears. What is it, we wonder, that moves him so deeply; has David's playing filled him with remorse at his guilty thoughts? Or is he mourning the loss of his own youth, now that a new leader has arisen? Whatever it is, David remains quite unaware of it; busily plucking his harp, he is just a young musician of the same realistic kind we know from Terbrugghen's picture. Rembrandt's attention and sympathy are centered on the unhappy king. Through the wonderful play of light on Saul's face, he tells us all he has learned in his lifetime about the strange ways of the human spirit.

Paintings like this demand a lot of thoughtful attention if we want to understand them completely. At any rate, most of the art buyers of Holland found them too "difficult" for their taste. They much preferred pictures of familiar things and experiences, such as the *Fort on a*

94

79. Steen. THE EVE OF SAINT NICHOLAS. About 1660–65. Rijksmuseum, Amsterdam

River by Jan van Goyen (figure 76), with its view of a distant town, its sailboats and wind-mills. There is nothing remarkable about this scene—it might be almost anywhere along the Dutch coast—and people loved it just because they knew it so well. Van Goyen, however, is less interested in the details than in the special mood of these low-lying "nether lands" that are always at the mercy of wind and water. His vast grey sky seems calm enough, yet it holds the threat of those same forces whose fury we had seen unleashed in Rembrandt's *Christ in the Storm*.

Like so many artists of seventeenth-century Holland, van Goyen was a specialist; he did nothing but landscapes of the type we have just seen. Other Dutch landscape painters favored different moods and different kinds of scenes. Our next picture (figure 77), *The Jewish Grave-yard*, is by the most famous of them all, Jacob van Ruisdael. Here again the forces of nature are the main theme. Although the setting is frankly imaginary, it is carried out with as much—perhaps even more—conviction than if it were an actual place. The thunderclouds passing over the wild and deserted countryside, the ruined building, the rushing stream that has forced its way between the ancient graves, all help to create a mood of deepest gloom. Nothing endures on this earth, Ruisdael tells us; time, wind, and water will grind it all to dust—not only the feeble works of man but trees and rocks as well. He must have felt that way about his own life, for his name appears on the tombstone nearest to us.

Another group of specialists were the "painters of things," whose works we call still lifes. In figure 78 you see a very fine one by Willem Claesz Heda, painted in 1634. Earlier masters had been interested in things, too (look at Holbein's *George Gisze*, figure 61), but only as part of a human subject. Why then, did the Baroque painters regard still lifes as good enough to put a frame around, and how did they decide what to put into such pictures? In our painting, the silver dish and the great glass goblet are fine and expensive pieces, interesting in them-selves; the oysters go with the wine in the goblet, and the lemon goes with the oysters. Are we perhaps meant to wonder why this elegant lunch was left uneaten? The silver dish has been up-set, and one of the goblets is broken, but the arrangement as a whole is too tasteful and well balanced to fit any kind of a story. What really "explains" it is the artist's interest in light and its reflections on these varied surfaces. It is this that stamps our still life not only as Baroque but as Dutch Baroque of the 1630's. Compare it with Rembrandt's *Christ in the Storm* done a year earlier: you may find it hard to believe that two paintings so different as these could have anything at all in common, yet they share a peculiar silvery tone—the light "feels" the same in both.

Before we conclude our discussion of the art of Holland, let us have a quick look at the genre specialists, painters of daily life among the burghers and peasantry. *The Eve of Saint Nicholas* by Jan Steen (figure 79) shows a family at Christmas time. Nicholas—the Dutch counterpart of Santa Claus—has just visited the children, dealing out presents and punish-ments; everybody is having a fine time except the bad boy to the left, who has received nothing

96

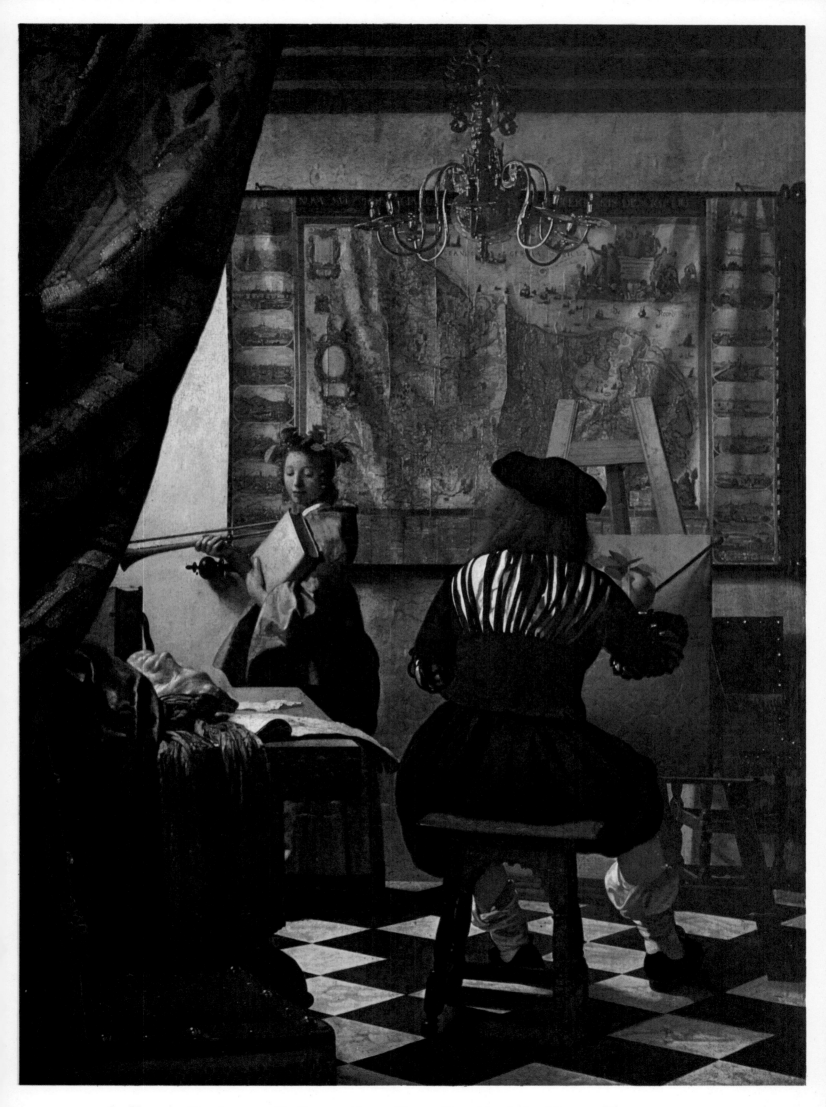

80. Vermeer. The Artist in His Studio. About 1665–70. Kunsthistorisches Museum, Vienna

but a birch rod (for punishment) in his shoe. Jan Steen has told this story with great relish, embroidering it with all sorts of warm human touches and delightful details. It all looks very much like the scene that is still acted out in our own homes every year. Few artists have made us feel the pleasures—and pains!—of family celebrations quite so well.

After the cheerful din of Steen's Christmas party, we are struck by the silence and order of *The Artist in his Studio* by Jan Vermeer (figure 80). Both pictures were done about the same time—in the 1660's—but this only helps to stress the basic difference between them. Steen, the story-teller, has the vivid sense of timing we know from Frans Hals. Vermeer, in contrast, shows us a timeless "still life" world, where nothing stirs, not even the figures. And yet, strange to say, they do not look at all frozen; it is rather as if this room, and everything in it, had been gently becalmed by some magic spell. The cool, clear daylight filtering in from the left provides all the action there is, and all that is needed, as it glances off the model's bright blue gown, sets the brass chandelier aglow, or settles in tiny, dew-like "droplets" on the curtain in the foreground. And now we realize the meaning of the spell: it makes us aware of the miracle of sight. Looking at this picture, we feel as if a veil had been pulled from our eyes, so that everything shines with a freshness and beauty we never knew before. In his early years Vermeer had learned a good deal from the painters of the Utrecht School; through them, he owes a debt to Caravaggio. But the quiet perfection of his style reminds us of something else— of Hubert and Jan van Eyck, the first great "discoverers of reality." In one sense, Vermeer completed what they had begun; yet he is also an important discoverer in his own right. Neglected until quite recently, he seems today far more modern in spirit than any other Dutch painter of his time.

In all of seventeenth-century art, there was only one other painter as completely devoted to the wonders of seeing as Vermeer: Diego Velázquez, certainly the greatest master of the Spanish Baroque. As a young man he, too, had come under the influence of Caravaggio's style: after he was appointed court painter to the King of Spain, he came to know Rubens and studied the works of Titian. His mature style, however, is unlike any of these. It can no more be "explained" than that of Vermeer. Most of Velázquez' works are royal portraits that had to follow set patterns, but every once in a while he would do a picture entirely on his own, such as *The Maids of Honor* of 1656 (figures 81, 82). It might also be called "the artist in his studio," for it shows Velázquez himself at work on a huge canvas, probably the very

81. Velázquez. THE MAIDS OF HONOR.

82. Velázquez. THE MAIDS OF HONOR (detail). 1656. Prado Museum, Madrid

picture we see before us. In the center is the little princess Margarita with her playmates and maids of honor. Her parents, the King and Queen, have just stepped into the room; their faces are reflected in the mirror on the back wall, which means that they saw the scene exactly as we do. In other words, Velázquez has painted a "king's-eye view" of his studio. But could the King and Queen really have seen *as much* here as Velázquez shows us? Were they as struck as we are by the soft, shadowy depth of the room? Did they sense the drama of the sunlight flooding the foreground the way we do? Velázquez' brushwork may at first glance remind you of Frans Hals, but you will find it a great deal more varied and subtle, for its aim is not to catch figures in motion but rather the movement of light *over* the figures. Light, to Velázquez, is what *makes* color and form; that's why he puts so many kinds of light into his picture—to find out how different they make things look; how the colors of a gown can change from warm to cool, and its "feel" from crisp to soft. If we had to pick a single work to sum up the "language" of Baroque painting, we could hardly make a better choice than *The Maids of Honor*.

Moving on from Spain to France, we find a very different taste at the royal court at Paris. King Louis XIV liked to be called the "Sun King," because he wanted it known that everything in France depended on his will, just as all life on earth depends on the sun. He even wanted to control the way French artists painted, and he did this through the Royal Academy, an official school for painters and sculptors. In the past young artists had always been trained by working in the shops of older men; during the Baroque era, this was still the usual method. But since the Renaissance, as we have seen, practical skill and experience were no longer enough for the artist. He needed to know a good deal of science and theory, too, so certain masters had founded private academies where they taught these things to groups of young artists. At the Royal Academy of Louis XIV, practice and theory were combined into a complete system of instruction, with the aim of giving the student an approved standard of style and beauty. This program became the model for all the later academies, and its echoes can still be felt among the art schools of today. Even so, it never worked very well. The most important thing in art, after all, is imagination, and it's pretty hard to make rules about that. Artists are by nature "unruly," so the best of them usually stayed outside the academies. In fact, the man on whose work the "ideal style" of the Royal Academy was based, preferred to live in Rome, at a safe distance from the pressure of the Court. He was Nicolas Poussin, the greatest French painter of the seventeenth century. *The Abduction of the Sabine Women* (figure 83) which he did in 1636–37, will show you why the Academy considered him such a perfect example for its students. The subject is a famous event from Early Roman times. In the beginning, there was a great shortage of women in Rome, since the city had been founded by an adventurous band of men from across the sea. The Romans tried to find wives among their neighbors, the Sabines, but the Sabine men would not let them. So they used a trick—having invited the entire Sabine tribe into the city for a peaceful festival, they suddenly fell upon them with arms and took the women away by force. Poussin was, of course, interested in this scene as a drama involving many different kinds of action and emotion. At the same time, however, he felt that it must be treated in a noble and heroic manner, so instead of trying to imagine how ordinary people would behave in such a situation he modeled his figures after Classical statues and after the masters of the Roman High Renaissance (compare Raphael's *Heliodorus* mural, figure 49). Still, Poussin was far from blind towards the art of his own day. The flowing movement in his picture reminds us of Rubens, and the light has some of the sharpness of Caravaggio's. Drawing and modeling were obviously more important to Poussin than painting—he believed in form as something apart from light and color—yet there is a fine color sense in the *Sabine Women*, and the soft and airy background landscape seems almost Venetian. The entire picture suggests an artist who knew his own mind almost

83. Poussin. THE ABDUCTION OF THE SABINE WOMEN. 1636–37. Metropolitan Museum of Art, New York

too well. Poussin's style did not just happen; it grew from conscious effort. His aim, it seems, was an art of the "golden middle ground" where form and color, thought and feeling, truth and beauty, the ideal and the real are in harmony with each other. Since all this involved such discipline and self-control, Poussin's style was considered more "teachable" than that of any other important master. Poussin himself wrote about his work at great length in his letters to friends or patrons. Sometimes he would discuss a single picture, explaining in detail exactly what he had done, and why; or he would set down theories and ideas about painting in general, always confident in his belief that art could be reasoned out like any other subject. The teachers at the Academy followed the same method of taking a picture apart as if it were an intricate piece of machinery. One of them even made up a sort of scoreboard of the great painters of all periods with definite grades for each one in composition, drawing, color, and "expression" (in the last Caravaggio got a zero, the lowest mark!). All this, of course, never produced another Poussin, yet we still admire his work and respect his ideals.

TOWARDS REVOLUTION

WHEN WE THINK of the eighteenth century, the things that come to our mind are, first of all, the American Revolution of 1776 and the French Revolution of thirteen years later. We are also apt to remember that it was the Age of Enlightenment, the time of the great social thinkers who believed that all human affairs ought to be ruled by reason and the common good—a revolution of the mind that started a good many years before the political revolutions. This is all true enough, yet it gives us a somewhat one-sided view of the times. It was indeed an age of change, but most of the changes happened slowly, rather than from one day to the next, and until the late years of the eighteenth century, life was not so very different from what it had been in the seventeenth. In art, too, the trends that had begun during the Baroque era continued for quite a long time without any violent breaks. Since we have seen before how freely new ideas in art could cross from one country to the next, it will no longer surprise us to find that we can trace the pageantry of Rubens, the realism of the Dutch masters, the severe ideals of Poussin, even when they appear in other places and under different circumstances.

In France, the early years of the century saw a really striking change of public taste. During the reign of Louis XIV, the Royal Academy had controlled much of the art life of the country, and the style of Poussin had been widely imitated. The "Sun King" had kept a stern eye upon the manners and living habits of his courtiers for over half a century. When he finally died in 1715, it was as if the entire French Court had decided to go on a holiday. The nobles deserted the Royal Palace of Versailles, where they had been forced to live before, and built themselves elegant private town houses in Paris. These they had decorated by artists who had broken with the old tradition of the Academy. Their hero was no longer Poussin but Rubens, who to them represented all the things the Academy had frowned upon: color, light, movement, and a frank pleasure in living. Antoine Watteau, who came from the

84. Boucher. SHEPHERD AND SHEPHERDESS. 1755. Louvre Museum

85. Watteau. MEZZETIN. About 1715. Metropolitan Museum of Art, New York

northern border of France near Flanders, was the first, and by far the most gifted, painter of this new era, which we often call the Rococo. His *Mezzetin* (figure 85), done about 1715, shows us Watteau's favorite subject, a character out of the popular comedy theater of the time. The easy, flowing brushwork, and the splendid color leave no doubt in our minds about the influence of Rubens, even though Watteau lacks the sweeping energy of the great Fleming. Instead, we find delicate, slender forms and a mood, half gay and half sad, that may remind you a bit of Giorgione's *Concert*. Watteau, however, has made the situation far more pointed: Mezzetin is an actor doomed to serenade his lady love without hope, both on the stage and in real life—we recognize him as a relative of those sorrowful clowns that have survived till today in such popular successes as the opera *I Pagliacci*.

Watteau's love of the theater gives us a clue to the spirit of Rococo society. It was, for the nobles at any rate, an age of play-acting—of pretending that their life was as free from worry as that of Francois Boucher's shepherd and shepherdess (figure 84), who live in a delightful world where the sheep never stray, so that they can spend all their time in the pursuit of love. Marie Antoinette, the last Queen of France, actually had a model farm built on the grounds of the Palace of Versailles, where she and her friends could play at being milkmaids and field hands when they got tired of the formality of court life.

There was, however, another side to French eighteenth-century painting, especially during

86. Greuze. THE VILLAGE BRIDE. 1761. Louvre Museum, Paris

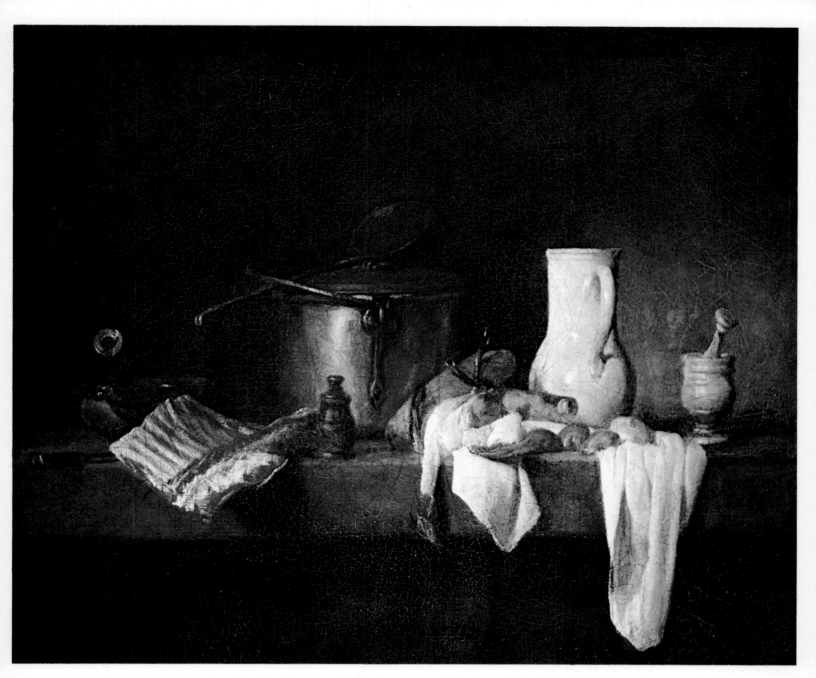

87. Chardin. Kitchen Still Life. 1735. Museum of Fine Arts, Boston

the thirty years preceding the Revolution. It reflects the growing importance of the common man, who, as the "citizen" of 1789, was to become the ruler of France. In 1761, while Boucher was still catering to the taste of the nobles with his powdery shepherds and shepherdesses, Jean-Baptiste Greuze did *The Village Bride* (figure 86), a subject drawn from the daily life of the people, which won him the praise of all the leading critics. He had been trained in the Rococo style, but here he breaks with his own past and turns to the realistic genre painters of Holland for inspiration. His reasons for picking a scene like this, however, were quite different from those of the Dutch masters. Steen's *Eve of Saint Nicholas* strikes us as a real event, observed with humor and sympathy, while *The Village Bride* is "staged" by actors. The bride looks too bashful, her mother too tear-stained, the grandfather too venerable to be quite convincing. We feel that Greuze wants to pull our heartstrings at all cost—"just look how touching, how sincere these poor people are!" he seems to say. Every detail in the picture plays a part in this message, even the hen with her chicks; one of them has left the brood and is sitting alone on the saucer to the right, just the way the bride is leaving *her* "brood." Sincere emotion has degenerated into bathos here. Strangely enough, *The Village Bride* was acclaimed as a masterpiece, and the loudest praise came from the most "enlightened" minds— from the advocates of the rule of reason. These men liked the fact that everything in Greuze's picture "meant" something, and that the artist wanted to appeal to our moral sense instead of just giving us pleasure like the Rococo painters. They overlooked, of course, that a worthy moral is not enough—in fact, it isn't even necessary—to make a great work of art.

We can learn this lesson from the *Kitchen Still Life* by Jean Siméon Chardin (figure 87). Its meaning is similar to Greuze's, but Chardin conveys it to us without preaching or acting, and yet far more effectively. Chardin, too, admired Dutch painting, and his picture comes from such earlier still lifes as the one by Willem Claesz Heda (figure 78). However, instead of using expensive silver dishes and hand-blown glass, he picked a few plain, sturdy kitchen pieces and some uncooked meat and fowl—the household things of the common man. Chardin has found so much intrinsic beauty in these simple everyday objects, he treats them with such respect and understanding, that they suddenly become important as symbols for a way of life. Somehow, we feel, his quiet and unassuming picture has attained all the dignity and simplicity that Greuze tried, in vain, to put into *The Village Bride*. And the reason is that Chardin speaks directly to us in the painter's own language—through color, light, and form—instead of borrowing the language of the stage.

During those years many Frenchmen had a great admiration for England. The English had

88. Gainsborough. ROBERT ANDREWS AND HIS WIFE. About 1750. Collection G. W. Andrews, Redhill, Surrey

89. Hogarth. THE GRAHAM CHILDREN. 1742. The Tate Gallery, London

gone through a time of political revolution in the seventeenth century; they had forced the King to hand most of his powers over to Parliament, so that the "common Englishman" already had a voice, although a limited one, in his own government. As a result, England became the envy of the continental nations. Its wealth was growing rapidly, the overseas colonies prospered, and the British navy and merchant fleet ruled the seas. Last but not least, the English had begun to play an important part in the fine arts.

Since the time of the Reformation, there had been little painting in England except portraits, and the leading artists had been foreigners: Holbein under Henry VIII, Flemings and Dutchmen later on. Even in the eighteenth century, when English artists came to the fore again, portraits were all they could count on for a steady living; but many of them did other

90. Copley. WATSON AND THE SHARK. 1778. Museum of Fine Arts, Boston

subjects as important sidelines, so that these, too, found a home in England. William Hogarth was such a painter. His particular interest lay in realistic scenes from daily life, similar to those of the Dutch genre masters. Hogarth, however, gave a keen satirical edge to these pictures and strung them together into series that told a story in many separate "installments." His sense of humor, as well as his fresh and observant eye, may also be seen in the delightful portrait of the Graham children (figure 89), done in 1742. It will remind you of Jan Steen's lively family in figure 79, even though Hogarth's colors are brighter and his brushwork freer. The picture is, of course, not meant to be a genre scene. We can guess from the fine costumes that the parents of these children must have been very well-to-do; they probably expected our artist to paint quite a formal portrait, with poses borrowed from adults. Hogarth has done that, but he has also found ways of relieving the stiffness of such a group. The two girls, we feel, are just having fun pretending to be ladies, and over on the right he tells us a little story—the boy is cranking his music-box for the bird in the cage, but a large cat has jumped onto the back of the chair, and the poor bird is so afraid of its greedy stare that instead of singing it only flaps its wings and shrieks.

The most famous portrait painter of eighteenth-century England, Thomas Gainsborough, had a sideline, too: he created wonderful landscapes. For instance, in his portrait of *Robert*

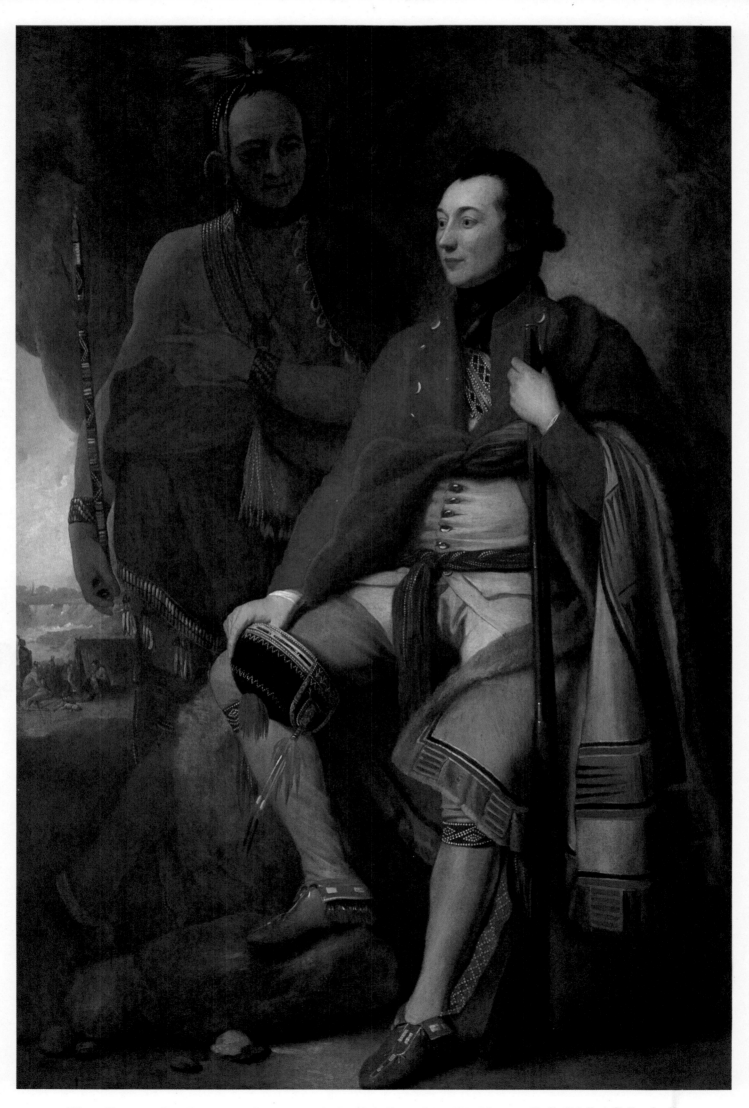

91. West. COLONEL GUY JOHNSON. About 1775. National Gallery of Art, Washington, D.C. (Mellon Collection)

92. David. THE DEATH OF MARAT. 1793. Royal Museum, Brussels

Andrews and His Wife (figure 88), he has made the outdoor setting as important as the sitters. The cloudswept view will remind you of Dutch landscapes, such as those in figures 76 and 77, but now the forces of nature seem gentle, rather than threatening. This land belongs to the country squire and his lady, and they, in a sense, belong to it. Gainsborough here suggests the charm of a country life that is real, not make-believe as in Boucher's picture (figure 84).

The North American colonies were by now old enough to have some fine painters of their own. The two most gifted ones, however, did not remain at home long enough to witness America's coming-of-age. Benjamin West, a Pennsylvania Quaker, and John Singleton Copley, from Boston, had gone to London a few years before the American Revolution. They had such success there that they stayed on for good, and West even became court painter to King George III and president of the British Royal Academy of Painting. This Academy was patterned on the principles of Poussin, but its ideals were much less severely Classical; in fact, they were broad enough to include the art of Rembrandt. West's portrait of *Colonel Guy Johnson* (figure 91), painted about 1775, is bathed in a light of Rembrandt-like warmth, although we miss the Dutch master's expressive force. The poses of the figures, on the other hand, seem a bit self-consciously heroic, as if the two were Ancient Romans, while the costumes, and all the other trappings, are faithfully observed, down to the last detail. Colonel Johnson was one of our first superintendents of Indian affairs. He is shown here with his trusted friend, Thayendanegea, who looks very much like "the noblest redskin of them all." West must have been quite proud of his American background, since he stressed all the little touches of frontier life (including the Indian encampment on the left) which no European painter could have known so well.

This sense of adventure may be found even more strikingly in Copley's *Watson and the Shark* (figure 90) of 1778. The picture is based on Mr. Watson's own account of his gruesome experience, which happened in the harbor of Havana and cost him a leg before he was pulled aboard the boat. Of course the scene did not look exactly as depicted here, but then Copley did not really mean to reconstruct it detail by detail. What he wanted was to make it as thrilling as possible, and he has used every trick of the Baroque style to this end. Caravaggio himself could hardly have "timed" it better. Yet behind all this we feel an imagination that carries the flavor of the New World rather than of the Old.

The American Revolution was fought for much the same reasons that were to bring on the Revolution in France: unfair taxes imposed on the people by a government in which they had no voice. It is one of the bitter jokes of history that the French King aided the Colonists' struggle for freedom, since he saw it as a chance to weaken the power of England. Their success may well have been the last bit of fuel that brought his own pot of political troubles to a boil. Criticism of the weak and corrupt government, and attacks on the holders of special privilege had been growing for a long time in France. We have seen signs of this in Greuze's *Village Bride*, where the honesty and goodness of the poor is meant to show up the moral decay of the aristocrats. Other painters went even further: they depicted the stories of heroic defenders of freedom in Ancient Athens or Rome, conveying the idea of "give me liberty or give me death." Even the style of these pictures carried a moral message. It was based on the severe, "ideal" style of Poussin, as a rebuke to painters like Boucher, who had modeled their works on those of Rubens and were now looked down upon as mere pleasure-seekers without anything worthwhile to say (it was at this time that the terms Baroque and Rococo came into use as unflattering labels). But the "anti-Rococo" painters were far more rigid than Poussin in their admiration for Ancient art, so that we speak of their work as Neo-Classic. Just as the artists of the Renaissance had helped to bring about a new era in science, so the Neo-Classic artists had a share in paving the way for the new political era that began with the French Revolution.

Among these men, the most important was Jacques Louis David, who took an active part in the Revolution and became its "official" painter. His picture of the *Death of Marat* (figure 92), done in 1793, is a memorial to one of the heroes of the struggle. David's deep emotion has made a masterpiece out of a scene that would have embarrassed many lesser artists, for Marat had been murdered in his bathtub. A painful skin disease caused him to do his paperwork there, with a wooden board serving as his desk. One day a young woman named Charlotte Corday burst in, handed him a personal petition, and while he read it plunged a knife into his chest. Whatever her side of the story—and Marat was hated by many—David makes us feel that this is no ordinary murder but something close to the death of a saint who gave his life for his faith—a saint of flesh and blood, like those of Caravaggio.

THE AGE OF MACHINES

THE FRENCH REVOLUTION had replaced the King with a republican government. The Republic, however, lasted only a decade. Before the century was out, France was again ruled by one man. Napoleon Bonaparte had risen to power as the leader of the Republican armies when the nation was attacked by its neighbors, who feared that the slogans of the Revolution—Liberty, Equality, and Fraternity—would soon catch on with their own people. The military genius of Napoleon conquered them all, except for England. He then made himself Emperor, a thousand years after Charlemagne. But in another ten years, in 1814, his army was beaten, and he was taken prisoner, by the united forces of England, Germany, and Russia.

Napoleon is another of the bitter jokes of history. In order to defeat him, the other countries had to take over a good part of the revolutionary ideas they had been so afraid of. For Napoleon did not undo the results of the Revolution; he simply used them for his own ends. His was the first modern army—a mass army of citizen soldiers fired by a feeling of patriotic duty. His enemies, who fought him at first only with soldiers hired for money, had to create mass armies, too; and having asked this common sacrifice of everybody, they found it more and more difficult to resist people's demands for more rights. Under Napoleon, a man rose in rank because of what he could do, not because he came from a noble family; here again the Emperor set an example to those countries where personal ability was less well rewarded. No wonder, then, that after the Napoleonic wars the common man felt greater confidence in his own powers and in his claim to those hard-won rights that Americans had been enjoying ever since 1776.

Napoleon fancied himself an Ancient Roman Emperor re-born. And the painters who, before and during the Revolution, had preached the heroic virtues of the Ancient republics, now took the elegance and splendor of Imperial Roman art as their model. David himself had been one of the earliest and most ardent admirers of Napoleon, but he no longer held the same commanding position as before; a number of younger artists, who had grown up with the Revolution, were now taking the lead. They included David's star pupil, Jean Auguste Domi-nique Ingres, whose wonderful portrait of *Madame Rivière* can be seen in figure 93. Notice how women's fashions have changed—instead of the billowing skirts of Baroque and

93. Ingres. MADAME RIVIÈRE. 1805. Louvre Museum, Paris

94. Goya. THE THIRD OF MAY, 1808 (THE SHOOTING OF CITIZENS OF MADRID BY NAPOLEON'S SOLDIERS). 1814-15. The Prado, Madrid

Rococo days (compare figures 70, 82, 88, and 89), Madame is wearing a simple gown that follows the natural outlines of the body. While not exactly like the costume of the Roman lady in the Boscoreale mural (figure 13), it does remind us of her. You will find these comparisons interesting in other ways, too. As a faithful believer in the Neo-Classic theories of David, Ingres regarded himself first of all as a draftsman and designer. Since he thought color and light less essential than form, he has carefully avoided the broad, flowing brushwork of the Baroque masters. Yet he was much more of a "painter's painter" than he thought. In his *Madame Rivière*, the colors are of extraordinary beauty and transparency, the surfaces have a delicate pearly sheen, and the poetic mood is as important as the finely balanced design in holding the picture together. Compared to the Boscoreale lady, our portrait seems almost photographic in the exact rendering of every detail. Here Ingres shows a concern for "truth" that also comes from David—we saw it in the *Death of Marat*—and that in lesser hands could easily become a dangerous liability. This desire of the time for exact likenesses had a good deal to do with the actual invention and development of photography between 1820 and 1840, when Ingres was at the height of his fame.

Meanwhile the Baroque-Rococo style, with its emphasis on imagination rather than "truth," and on light and color rather than form, had never died out completely. There were artists in Napoleon's day who painted Neo-Classic ideas in a Baroque way, while others took over the Neo-Classic language but used it for highly imaginative, even fantastic subjects. One very important painter, the Spaniard Francisco Goya, even managed to turn the Baroque into a "modern" style without being touched by the Neo-Classic trend at all. Like Velázquez, whose art he greatly admired, Goya was the official painter of the Spanish King, although from the very start he did a great many things besides court portraits. Perhaps his most powerful works are those devoted to the struggle of the Spanish people against the army of Napoleon, which had occupied the country but never really conquered it. In *The Third of May, 1808* (figure 94) he shows the shooting of a group of Madrid citizens who had resisted the foreign invaders. The blazing color, the broad "handwriting" in paint, the dramatic light, all remind us of the Baroque. Why then do we feel so strongly that the picture belongs to the early nineteenth century in spirit? The subject itself, of course, is new and daring, but the way Goya has treated it is even more so. David's *Marat* had reminded us of a religious painting; *The Third of May, 1808* makes equally full use of the devices of religious art—Goya had been deeply impressed with the work of Rembrandt—and again people are dying, not for the Kingdom of Heaven but for Liberty. For Goya, however, the real tragedy was that the shooting should be done by the French. Like so many others he had thought at first that the forces of Napoleon would carry the ideals of the Revolution into his own backward country. *The Third of*

May, 1808 is a memorial to shattered hopes—and to those of countless others in the years to come. This same scene has been repeated so many times since Goya's day, always with a different cast of characters and in countries all over the globe, that it has become a terrifying symbol of the "era of revolutions."

Let us now turn to the *Mounted Officer of the Guard* (figure 96), to see how a young French French painter felt about Napoleon. This life-size picture was done in 1812 by the marvelously talented Théodore Géricault, then only twenty-one years of age, as a sort of ideal portrait of the Napoleonic soldier. Born more than four decades after David and Goya, Géricault had a viewpoint very different from either. For him, politics no longer had the force of a faith; all he saw in the Emperor's military campaigns was the color and swirling excitement of violent action. These, of course, were just the things that could not be well expressed in the Neo-Classic style, so our artist has gone all the way back to Rubens for his source of inspiration (compare the dramatic *Crucifixion* by the older master in figure 69). Goya had still been raised in the tradition of Baroque art; Géricault revived it, as the style best suited to his own temper. With him we meet a new type of painter, and an important and vital new movement in art called Romantic.

The word actually comes from the field of literature, where "romances" (that is, stories of adventure) were very popular at that time, so that it describes a state of mind rather than a particular style of painting. Few Romantic painters came as close to the full-blown Baroque as Géricault in his *Mounted Officer,* but they all shared a similar outlook. Art to them did not mean a fixed ideal, the way it did to the Neo-Classic artists. There was no such thing as a single "perfect" style for them. What mattered in art and in life, they felt, was not the *kind* of experience you had but how strongly you felt about it. One might almost say that the Romantics sought emotion for emotion's sake. They believed in living dangerously, or at least thrillingly (and sometimes theatrically). Géricault, for instance, was an ardent horseman and died after a bad fall at the early age of thirty-three. As born rebels against any kind of set rules or values, the only thing they held sacred was the individual personality; and since they could not express

95. Delacroix. Arab Attacked by a Lion. About 1850.
The Art Institute of Chicago

96. Géricault. Mounted Officer of the Guard. 1812. Louvre Museum, Paris

97. Turner. THE FIGHTING TEMERAIRE TOWED TO HER LAST BERTH. 1838. The National Gallery, London

anybody's viewpoint but their own, people often found them hard to understand. In fact, the Romantics enjoyed being misfits in the society of their time. Here, then, you see the beginning of a split between artist and public that still persists today.

Just before Géricault's death, another fine Romantic painter appeared on the Paris scene:

118

98. Constable. HAMPSTEAD HEATH (sketch). 1821.
City of Manchester Art Galleries, England

Eugène Delacroix. He and Ingres were to be the two opposite poles of French painting until well past the middle of the century—they were "professional enemies," so to speak. At first Ingres, the great conservative, received all the honors and prizes, although Delacroix caught up with him in the end, when people had grown used to the Romantic movement. His *Arab Attacked by a Lion* (figure 95), done about 1850, still has a great deal in common with Géricault's *Officer*. Here again you find the Rubens-like energy of movement, the open, flowing brushwork, the thrill of violent action. By now the glamorous days of Napoleon and his Empire were only a dim memory, so that Delacroix had to go either to literature and history or, as in this case, to remote places for the kind of subject that excited his imagination. He had actually visited the Arabic world of North Africa once, but our scene is freely invented without any models.

In earlier years, both Géricault and Delacroix had been much impressed by English painting. England, where Romantic literature had had its start, had produced an important group of landscape painters at the beginning of the nineteenth century, all of them Romantic in temper. What Rubens was to the French Romantics, the Dutch Baroque landscape masters were to these Englishmen. In them they found a feeling, similar to their own, for the majestic forces of nature and for man's loneliness and insignificance when faced with these forces. Even so, they did not simply imitate their models, any more than the French copied Rubens. You can tell this from the view of *Hampstead Heath* (figure 98) by John Constable, painted towards 1830. The picture is one of the countless oil sketches, none of them much larger than this page, that Constable did of this district, which today is a suburb of London. They were done very quickly and on the spot, a new and unusual idea at the time; that is why our picture looks so different from van Goyen and Ruisdael (figures 76 and 77). The Baroque masters had never painted landscapes out-of-doors, even when they wanted to depict a particular place. They only made drawings, which they could then work up in the studio at their leisure. Constable, however, was so fascinated by the ever-changing moods of nature that these changes became far more important to him than the things that stayed the same about a given view. In the sketch reproduced here, he has caught a particularly splendid moment—a great sky drama of wind, sunlight, and clouds, played over a vast sweep of countryside. The details on the ground are no more than the "backdrop," so they are barely indicated. Perhaps the scene did not look quite as exciting in reality, but since Constable's realization of it is the only account we have, we see it through his eyes and believe him.

With William Turner, the other great English landscapist of Constable's time, we often find believing rather more difficult. In *The Fighting Temeraire* (figure 97) of 1838, he

99. Hicks. THE PEACEABLE KINGDOM. About 1830. Worcester Art Museum, Mass.

100. Bingham. Fur Traders on the Missouri. About 1845. Metropolitan Museum of Art, New York

shows us a famous old warship, once the pride of the British fleet, being towed to her last berth against the light of a brilliant sunset. These fireworks in the sky are like a last salute at the burial of a dead hero who is going down in glory, like the sun itself. Let us also take note (because Turner intended us to) of the contrast beween the squat, monster-like tugboat and the silvery tallness of the *Temeraire*. All this is a splendid show, but it may make some of us feel a bit uncomfortable. Like an over-zealous organist, Turner has pulled a few stops too many, so that the music becomes deafening.

Landscape painting was perhaps the most original part of the Romantic movement in art. At any rate, it was the most popular. While Constable and Turner, each in his own way, show us the Romantic view of nature more clearly than anyone else, we find many others all over Europe doing similar things until far into the second half of the century. The New World, too, had its Romantic landscape artists, even though most Americans were far too busy coping

121

101. Homer. BREEZING UP. 1873–76. National Gallery of Art, Washington, D. C.
Gift of the W. L. and May T. Mellon Foundation

with nature in practical ways to pay much attention to the poetry of her moods. There were few painters among the people who settled the wilderness of the Middle West and Far West. Yet every once in a while these men would do pictures like the *Fur Traders on the Missouri* (figure 100) by George Caleb Bingham, full of the vastness and silence of the wide-open spaces. The two trappers in their dugout canoe with the black fox chained to the prow, soundlessly gliding downstream in the misty sunlight, carry us right back to the river life of Mark Twain's childhood, to Tom Sawyer and Huck Finn.

Winslow Homer's *Breezing Up* (figure 101), done about thirty years later than the *Fur*

122

Traders, was painted "down East" rather than in frontier country, but it shows just as fine a feeling for the great outdoors of America. Here, we are off the coast of New England at high noon on a fine, windy day, and we can almost smell the salty tang of the sea air as we sail along with the old fisherman and the three boys towards the distant lighthouse on the left, while the schooner follows its own steady course off to the right.

Bingham and Homer were talented professional artists, trained in the big cities of the East. Neither of them, we may be sure, had ever heard of Edward Hicks, the Pennsylvania preacher and sign painter who did *The Peaceable Kingdom* (figure 99). Hicks was a folk artist, a man of simple mind and simple faith, to whom painting was still a craft, and the Bible the Word of God, the way it had been to people in the Middle Ages. Like them, too, Hicks had a compelling imagination. His picture illustrates the words of the Prophet Isaiah about the coming of peace among men: "The wolf shall dwell with the lamb, and the leopard shall lie down with the kid . . . the cow and the bear shall feed together . . . and the lion shall eat straw like the ox." On the left we see William Penn signing his treaty with the Indians, a practical example of peacemaking, but it is the animals that really impress us. The ferocious lion chewing on his mouthful of straw beside the mild-eyed ox, the sly wolf, the leopard spread out like a fur rug, are all doing their best to live up to the sacred text. And if we smile at the way they act out their roles, we are also touched by their seriousness and sincerity.

But let us return from the Pennsylvania countryside to the noise and unrest of the mid-nineteenth century. In the years since the French Revolution, another and even greater revolution had been going on everywhere: the revolution in industry that came with the use of machines. There had, of course, been machines all along, but their usefulness had been limited because they could be run only by wind power (which was unreliable) or water power (which had to be used on the spot). The invention of the steam engine in the late eighteenth

102. Courbet. THE STONE BREAKERS. 1849. Picture Gallery, Dresden

century changed all that. Now the knowledge that natural scientists had been gathering ever since the Renaissance could be put to practical use in thinking up machines for an endless variety of purposes. This, in turn, led to more scientific discoveries and more inventions, right down to the technical miracles of our own time.

It is hard for us today to realize how completely steamboats, railroads, and factories unsettled everybody's way of life a hundred years ago. People marveled at the flood of cheap and plentiful goods made or shipped with the aid of machines, but the same machines also caused a good deal of human misery. The trained craftsmen of old were thrown out of work and their places taken by masses of industrial workers, unskilled, badly paid, and crowded together in unhealthy slums. No wonder the machine was welcomed by some as a blessing while others called it a curse. Altogether, the rise of modern industry overthrew a great many beliefs, habits, and institutions. It created new tensions and conflicts, yet at the same time it made people more dependent on each other's labor than ever before.

And what of the painters? What effect did the new thinking and new ways of life brought about by the Age of Machines have on them? The Romantics had put free-

103. Manet. THE FIFE PLAYER. 1866. Louvre Museum

104. Manet. In the Boat. 1874. Metropolitan Museum of Art, New York

dom of feeling and imagination above anything else; but others thought this was just an easy way to escape from the realities of the time. They believed that in a period of scientific, social, and industrial progress, art should only deal with contemporary subjects. In 1848, when a wave of revolutions swept over Europe, inspired by the demand of the lower classes for higher wages, better living conditions, and a more democratic society, these Realists began to portray the life of workers and peasants in a serious spirit. Their leader was Gustave Courbet, whose *Stone Breakers* (figure 102), painted in 1849, started an uproar similar to the one caused by Caravaggio two and a half centuries earlier. Here we find no "noble ideals," no flights of fancy, only an old man breaking up rocks, aided by his young helper. We learn little about them as persons, since their faces are turned away from us, yet we feel sympathy and respect for them right away because they are so firmly and monumentally *there*. The modern artist, Courbet believed, must stay firmly on the ground of everyday life; he must paint only what he can see directly, not what appears in his mind's eye; he should try to rival the old masters, but only in ambition, not by imitating them.

125

105. Renoir. LE PONT NEUF. 1872. Collection Mrs. Robert Boggs, New York

Even so, Courbet's own painting technique still reminds us a good deal of the seventeenth century. He was more interested in the new things he wanted to say than in finding a new way to say them. This new way had to be discovered by another great French painter, Edouard Manet. He also shared Courbet's idea that one should paint only what the eye actually sees, but he felt that in order to accomplish this he first had to re-think the whole language of painting. So he began by learning everything he could about this language; he made copies

126

and studies after the old masters, and for several years these "pictures of pictures" were his main concern. You can see the new language Manet worked out for himself if you compare his *Fife Player* of 1866 (figure 103) with the *Stone Breakers*. Since the Late Middle Ages when pictures first became "windows," painters had always relied on modeling and shading to make their shapes look round and solid, and the spaces around the shapes deep and hollow. Courbet, too, still painted that way. Manet, on the other hand, decided that all this could be done through differences in color alone, rather than through different shades of light and dark. In his *Fife Player*, the light hits the forms head-on, so that we

106. Bouguereau. YOUTH. About 1875

find practically no shadows, and no shading. The whole picture is made up of separate, flat color patches placed next to each other on the canvas. And every patch, whether it stands for a thing (such as a part of the boy's uniform) or just for empty space (like the light grey "patch" around the figure) has a clearcut shape of its own. What does all this mean? Simply this: that for Manet the picture has become more important than the things it represents. The limited world of the canvas, he found, has its own "natural laws," and the first of these is that every brush stroke, every color patch is equally "real," no matter what it stands for in nature. Vermeer and Velázquez had come closest to this idea of "pure painting" among the old masters. It remained for Manet, however, to turn the Baroque triumph of light into a triumph of color.

In the Boat (figure 104), done eight years after the *Fife Player*, shows you the next stage of the revolution Manet had started. Stimulated by younger artists (Claude Monet and others), who had carried his ideas further in their own canvases, Manet had turned to outdoor scenes such as this, flooded with sunlight of a brightness that makes all earlier paintings seem murky by comparison. Color is everywhere, especially in the shadows (if we can call them that!). It is a genre picture, but Manet gives us only a casual glimpse of the two people and what they are doing; his brushwork has become quick and sparkling like that of Hals or Constable (compare figures 72 and 98), so that the entire scene seems in motion. It was this that made the conservative critics call the new style

127

107. Degas. MANET. Drawing. About 1865.
Metropolitan Museum of Art, New York

Impressionism; since to their eyes such pictures were at best no more than quick impressions, unfinished sketches not worthy of serious attention. Moreover, they complained, the color was so raw that it hurt their eyes (they probably never went out on sunny days). One of the younger Impressionists, Auguste Renoir, was particularly successful in using the technique of Impressionism to catch the bustling life of the Paris streets, as you can see in his *Pont Neuf* (figure 105) of 1872. It shows one of the bridges over the river Seine in the blazing noonday sun of mid-summer, and again it is the wealth and brilliance of color that gives the picture such charm and gaiety. The air quivers with the heat reflected from the pavement, but the shade seems deliciously cool—altogether, a perfect day for a stroll.

How could anyone have failed to be captivated by the wonderful freshness of this scene? Yet for most people during those years the greatest living painter was William Adolphe Bouguereau. He, and his countless imitators, were awarded all the official honors, and his pictures sold for prices as high as those paid for the rarest of old masters. Figure 106 shows you one of his works, to which he gave the title *Youth*. The painting depicts a vapid and coy young woman clothed in "historically correct" Classical garb, leaning against an "Ancient Roman" fountain, and playfully beset by two fluttering, curly-headed cupids, the "voices of love." Maybe there is nothing wrong with this idea as such—after all, Botticelli's *Birth of Venus* (figure 44) also has a rather complicated poetic theme, and of a similar kind. The reason Bouguereau's painting has lost most of its appeal for us, while Botticelli's *Venus* and Renoir's *Pont Neuf* have kept theirs, may be that Bouguereau was not very sensitive to the beauty of painted shapes and colors; he was satisfied simply to "photograph" his model, a job that the camera could have done just as well and much more conveniently. Perhaps that is why people liked his work so: they trusted it the way they trusted the camera, which "never lies," and were quite willing to see inspiration where we today can find only perspiration and cheap sentiment.

Bouguereau shows us the style of the art academies at its worst. He thought of himself as the guardian of the Classical spirit, the heir of Ingres and David (and, through them, of Poussin and Raphael), but he simply did not know how to practice what he preached. Still, the academic "system" out of which he came was not wholly bad; a young artist of real talent

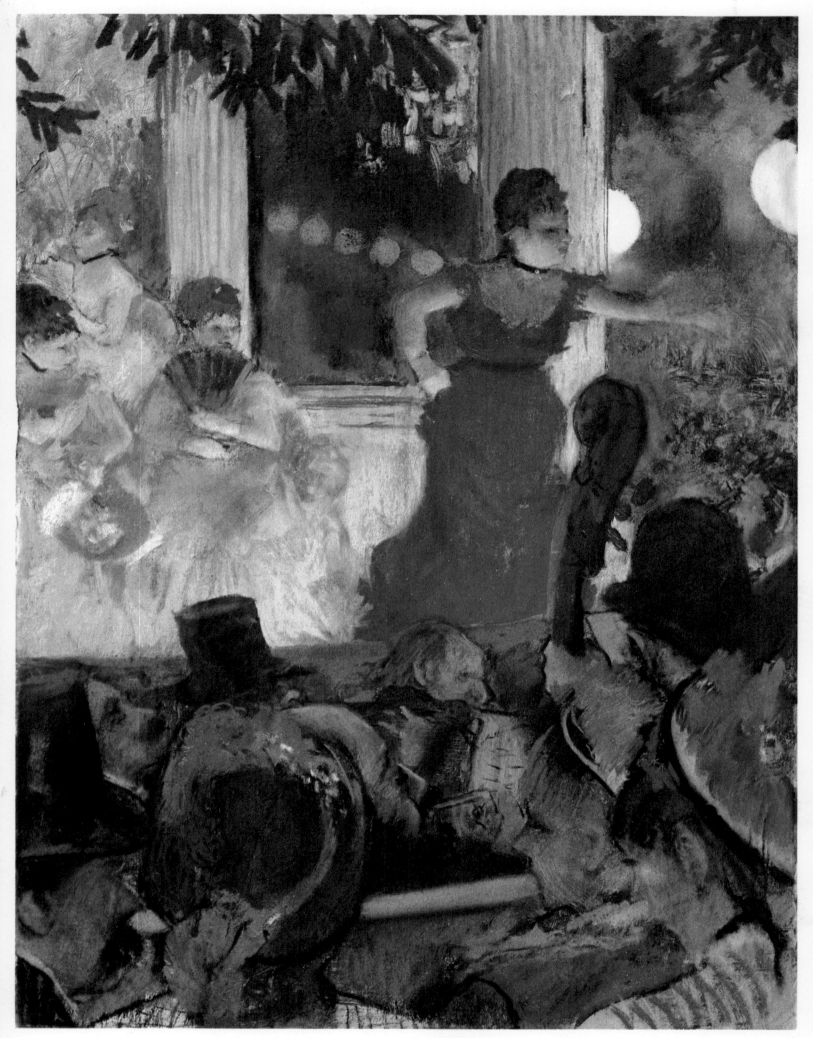

108. Degas. Café Concert: At Les Ambassadeurs. 1876–77. Museum, Lyons

could profit from it despite its glaring faults. One of the great masters of Impressionism, Edgar Degas, had gone through this kind of training. He had studied with a follower of Ingres, and had come away with a respect for line and composition that served him well throughout his life. The splendid portrait drawing (figure 107) that Degas made of his friend Manet about 1865, not long after their first meeting, is far closer to the spirit of Ingres than anything Bouguereau ever created, even though at first glance it may not strike you as Classical at all. The pose, to be sure, seems casual and relaxed, as if Degas had caught his sitter unawares, yet the figure is carefully composed, and the lines are so graceful, the forms so cleanly set down, that we need not be afraid to compare them with Ingres' *Madame Rivière* (figure 93).

Unlike other members of the group around Manet, Degas hardly ever painted out-of-doors. Among the favorite subjects of this "indoors and night-time Impressionist" were scenes of the theater and show business, such as the *Café Concert* (figure 108) of 1876–77. Here the bright colors of the costumes, the dramatic lighting, the contrast between the "artificial" world of the stage and the "real" world of the spectators, have been woven into a wonderfully rich and vivid pattern. Again we get what seems to be almost a chance view, as if the artist had sketched it in a few minutes' time while passing through the crowded hall.

109. Cézanne. HOUSE IN PROVENCE. 1885–86. The John Herron Art Institute, Indianapolis, Indiana

110. Cézanne. FRUIT BOWL, GLASS, AND APPLES. 1879-82. Collection M. René Lecomte, Paris

Actually, however, this unstudied, off-center look hides a lot of hard work and exact planning. Notice, for instance, how the string of lanterns to the left of the singer in the red dress helps to draw attention to her outstretched arm; how the neck of the bass fiddle sticks out of the orchestra pit in exactly the right spot to make us realize the gap in space between foreground and background. The way the picture is put together shows all the care of an Old Master, but an Old Master with a thoroughly modern mind.

Among the earliest admirers of Manet was a rather gruff young man from the south of France named Paul Cézanne. He quickly took over and assimilated the new language of such pictures as *The Fife Player* and made it the basis of his own work. In the early 1870's Cézanne began to do brightly lit outdoor scenes similar to Manet's *In the Boat* and Renoir's *Pont Neuf*, but he never shared his friends' interest in the "spur of the moment," in movement and change; and towards 1880 he left Impressionism behind and became the first of the Post-Impressionists. This is not a very telling label for the mature Cézanne, or for those who were in sympathy with his efforts, but at least it suggests that they were not "anti-Impressionists." All these men knew how much they owed to the revolution that Manet had brought on; they were certainly not trying to undo it. On the contrary, they wanted to carry it further in various directions, so that Post-Impressionism was actually just a later stage—though a very important one—of the same basic "Manet Revolution," as we might call it.

Let us see now what kind of Post-Impressionism Cézanne had arrived at. His still life, *Fruit Bowl, Glass, and Apples* (figure 110), has the freshness of color and the free brushwork we have come to expect of an Impressionist picture, but after you look at it for a while you will notice all sorts of puzzling things. There are dark outlines drawn around most of the shapes, and the shapes themselves have been made simpler than they would be in nature; the table top seems to tilt upwards, and the foreshortening of the bowl and glass is not "correct." Also, the colors seem to follow a scheme that stresses the contrast of cool and warm tones, and the brush strokes form a sort of pattern that runs over the entire canvas and gives it a shimmering effect. Has Cézanne done all this on purpose, or didn't he know any better? Curiously enough, the longer we study the picture, the more we come to feel that these things look "right" in it, although they are "wrong" according to nature. And that is exactly what Cézanne wanted us to feel. For him, even more than for Manet, a framed canvas was a separate world, with laws of its own that were more important to him than the laws of nature; he could not take something out of nature and put it into a picture without changing it so as to make it fit in. "Bowls, glasses, and fruit," he seems to be telling us, "are not at all remarkable in themselves. We see them every day. They become remarkable only because of what I do with them in my picture. That is my task, my challenge as an artist." But Cézanne did not think of nature simply as his raw material, to be dealt with as he pleased. He had the greatest respect for it and did not change it any more than he felt he had to. In his *Fruit Bowl*, and perhaps even more so in the slightly later *House in Provence* (figure 109), you can see how delicately he has balanced the claims of art and nature: his forms are arranged in depth, yet they also cling to the surface; they are simpler and clearer than in nature, since the world of painting is a limited and orderly one, made up of color patches rather than of atoms. The forms are carefully related to each other and to the size of the canvas, yet they always remain

132

111. Seurat. A Sunday Afternoon on the Grande Jatte. 1884–86. The Art Institute of Chicago

part of the larger world outside, which does not stop at the frame of the picture.

Cézanne once explained that his aim was "to do Poussin over again, but from nature," which means that he wanted an art as solid and monumental as that of the Old Masters, without giving up what he had learned from Impressionism. The same words might be used to describe the work of Georges Seurat, another great Post-Impressionist. Seurat's career was as brief as those of Masaccio, Giorgione, and Géricault—he died in 1891 at the age of thirty-two—and what he achieved in so short a time is just as astonishing. His main efforts went into a few very large paintings, on each of which he spent a year's time or more. One

133

reason why he worked so slowly was his belief that art ought to be based on a "system"; like Degas, he had studied with a follower of Ingres, and his interest in theory came from this experience. But as with all artists of genius, Seurat's theories do not explain his pictures; it is the pictures, rather, that explain the theories.

In *A Sunday Afternoon on the Grande Jatte* (figure 111) Seurat has picked a subject popular among the Impressionists—a gay crowd enjoying a summer day on an island near Paris. The colors are of the same rainbow-brightness we saw in Renoir's *Pont Neuf*, but otherwise the picture is the very opposite of a quick "impression." Seurat, even more than Cézanne, sought to regain calmness and monumentality in painting, and he knew that this could be done only by bringing the strictest kind of order into the confused, shifting scene, by putting everything in the right place and making it stay there. The *Grande Jatte* is surely one of the most completely "thought-through" pictures of all time, as perfectly controlled as a mural by Piero della Francesca (compare figure 38); in fact, it has a timeless dignity that is matched only by the art of ancient Egypt (figure 6). This passion for order can be seen even in the brushwork. Cézanne's brush strokes, despite their regular, pattern-like quality, still betray a strongly personal touch; with Seurat, every stroke has become a precise little dot of pure color, a tiny, impersonal "building block" in the construction of the picture (this technique is known as Pointillism).

While Cézanne and Seurat were making a more severe, Classical art out of the Impressionist style, Vincent van Gogh led the way in a different direction; he believed that Impressionism did not allow the artist enough freedom to express his inner feelings. Since these were his main concern, he is sometimes called an Expressionist. Van Gogh, too, wanted to "re-do the Old Masters from nature," but his heroes were Delacroix and Rembrandt rather than Ingres and Poussin. Although he was to become the first great Dutch painter since the seventeenth century, van Gogh did not start out as an artist at all. His early interests were literature and religion; for a while he even worked as a lay preacher among the poor. Only in 1880, at the age of twenty-seven, did he turn to art, and since he died ten years later, his career was even shorter than that of Seurat. Almost all of his important works, in fact, date from the last three years of his life, which he spent mostly in the south of France. Towards the end, he began to suffer from fits of mental illness that made it more and more difficult for him to paint. De-

112. Van Gogh. PORTRAIT OF A PEASANT. Drawing. 1888.
Fogg Museum of Art, Cambridge, Massachusetts

113. Van Gogh. ROAD WITH CYPRESSES. 1889. Kröller-Müller State Museum, Otterlo, Holland

spairing of a cure, he finally decided to kill himself, for he felt very deeply that it was only his art that made life worth living for him.

The drawing, *Portrait of a Peasant* (figure 112), is filled with the same sense of pity that had impelled van Gogh to religious work among the poor in earlier years. The strongly modeled face stands out with incredible force, since everything else (the background, the hat, the shoulders) has been kept flat, for contrast. In this way the artist compels us to share his own experience, to feel what he felt—the look of inner pain in the eyes, the strange expression of the mouth with its weak, frozen smile. Like Cézanne and Seurat, van Gogh re-shapes nature, but for very different reasons. They stress the typical qualities of things; he picks out what is unique. With them, the artist tends to disappear behind his work; with him, every shape reveals his personal feelings. Where they seek balance and stability, he creates movement. Look, for instance, at the dots in the background of our drawing: they reflect the Pointillism of Seurat, but instead of staying in place they seem to be flowing this way and that, as if they had a will of their own. Elsewhere in the drawing, this same flow of the pen strokes becomes stronger still.

In the *Road with Cypresses* (figure 113) the personal "handwriting" of van Gogh is done with the brush, but every stroke stands out just as boldly, and his passion for movement is almost overpowering. The road streams past us, the trees lick upwards like flames, and the sky is filled with the whirling motion of the sun, moon, and stars. This magnificent vision of the unity of all forms of life again expresses van Gogh's religious feeling—a feeling as deep and strong as the faith of the Middle Ages, even though it is based on a belief in the creative force within nature, rather than on the Christianity of the Bible.

114. Gauguin. Offerings of Gratitude (Maruru). Woodcut.
About 1891–93. Museum of Modern Art, New York

136

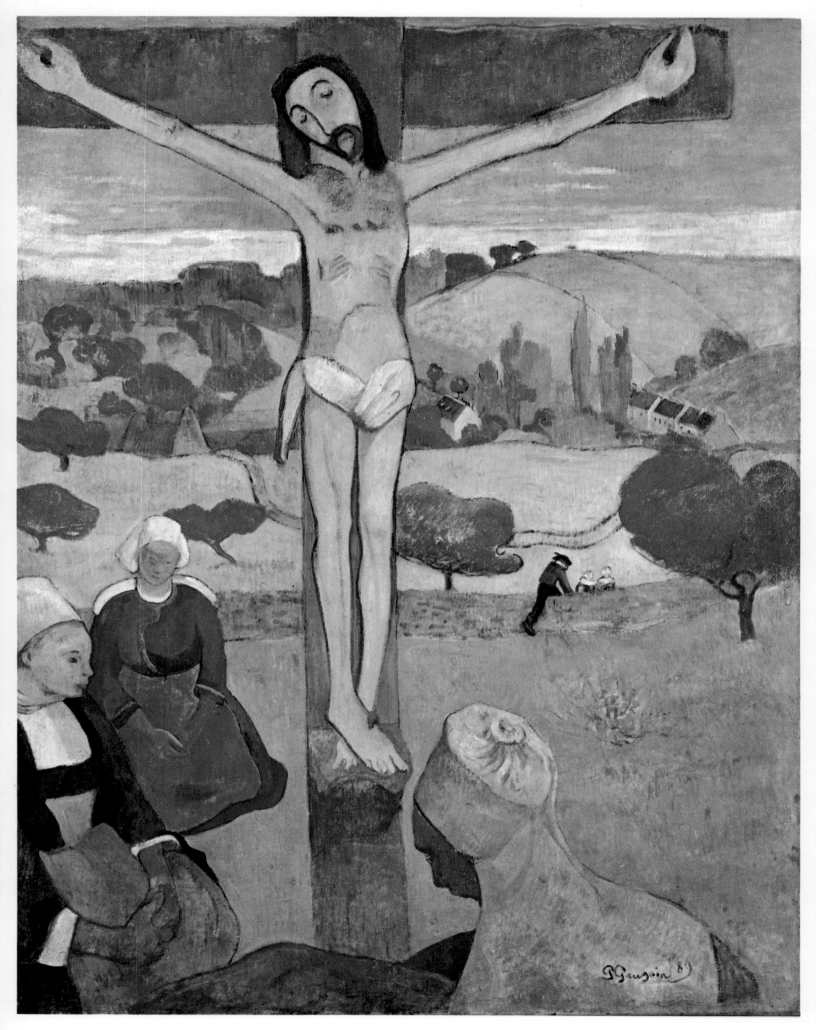

115. Gauguin. THE YELLOW CHRIST. 1889. Albright-Knox Art Gallery, Buffalo, New York

116. Munch. THE SCREAM. 1893. National Gallery, Oslo, Norway

Religion also played an important part in the work (if not in the life) of Paul Gauguin, who decided to turn artist even later in his career than van Gogh did. Until the age of thirty-five, Gauguin was a prosperous business-man who painted and collected modern pictures on the side (he once owned Cézanne's *Fruit Bowl, Glass, and Apples*). By 1889, however, he had founded a new movement in art that he called Symbolism. This style, though less in-tensely personal than van Gogh's, was in some ways an even bolder jump be-yond the bounds of Impressionism. Gauguin felt very strongly that Western civilization was "out of joint"; that our industrial society had forced men into an incomplete kind of life devoted to making money, while their emotions lay neglected. In order to rediscover this hidden world of feeling for himself, Gauguin went to live among the peasants of Brittany, in western France. He was particularly struck by the fact that religion still formed part of the every-day life of these country people, and in his *Yellow Christ* (figure 115) he has tried to express this simple and direct faith. The Christ is of a Late Gothic type, but on the level of folk art, since that is the way the three peasant women in the foreground think of Him. The other forms, too, have been simplified and flattened out, so as to stress that they are imagined, not observed from nature, and the brilliant colors are

138

117. Toulouse-Lautrec. AT THE MOULIN ROUGE. 1892. The Art Institute of Chicago

equally "un-natural." Gauguin's Symbolist style owes a good deal to medieval art (the *Yellow Christ* strongly reminds us of a piece of stained glass like the one in figure 21), yet there is one big difference: since he did not share the religious experience of the peasants, Gauguin could only paint pictures *about* faith, rather than *from* faith.

Two years later, Gauguin's search for the unspoiled life led him even farther afield. He went to the South Pacific island of Tahiti, as a sort of "missionary in reverse" who wanted to learn from the natives instead of teaching them. Gauguin spent almost ten years in this tropical setting, yet none of the pictures he painted there is as daring as the *Yellow Christ*. The most interesting works of this period are his woodcuts; in their frankly "carved" look and bold white-on-black patterns we can feel the influence of the native art of the South Seas. The one called *Offerings of Gratitude* (figure 114) again has religious worship for its theme, but now the image of a local god has taken the place of Christ.

Meanwhile, the ideas developed by Gauguin were taken up by other artists of the 1890's, among them the important Norwegian painter Edvard Munch. In *The Scream* (figure 116), Munch makes us "see" what it feels like to be afraid. It is a true picture of fear, the kind of terrifying fear without reason that grips us after we wake up from a nightmare. The long, wavy lines seem to carry the echo of the scream into every corner of the picture—earth and sky have become one great sounding board of fear.

There is a curiously haunted feeling about figure 117, too, even though it shows the inside of a well-known Paris nightspot, the Moulin Rouge in Montmartre. Henri de Toulouse-Lautrec, the artist who painted this picture, was a great admirer of Degas, but he also knew van Gogh and Gauguin. *At the Moulin Rouge* still has a good deal in common with Degas' Impressionist *Café Concert* (figure 108); there is the same sudden jump from foreground to background, the same contrasty lighting, the same interest in the gestures and poses of the performers. But Toulouse-Lautrec sees right through the gay surface of the scene. He views it with a cartoonist's sharp eye for character, including his own—he is the tiny, bearded man next to the very tall one in the back of the room. The large patches of flat color, on the other hand, with their dark, curving outlines, remind us of Gauguin. Toulouse-Lautrec was no Symbolist, and yet his picture means more than an Impressionist café scene. Whether he intended to or not, the artist makes us feel that this is a place of evil.

In 1886, there appeared in an exhibition of Post-Impressionist works some extraordinary pictures by a painter nobody had heard of before. His name was Henri Rousseau, and he turned

140

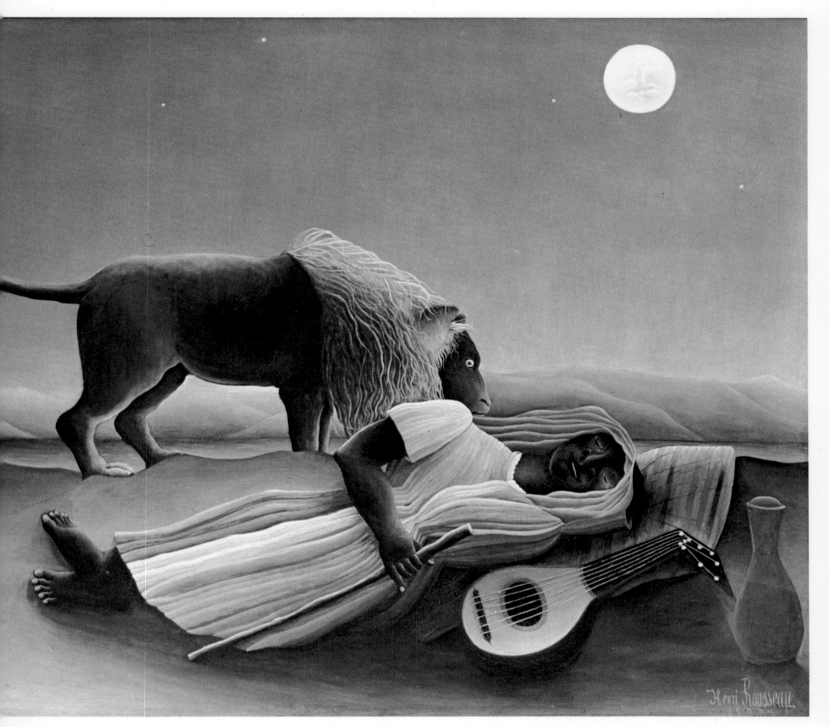

118. Henri Rousseau. THE SLEEPING GYPSY. 1897. Museum of Modern Art, New York. Gift of Mrs. Simon Guggenheim

out to be a retired customs official who had just started to paint, without training of any sort, at the age of forty. Rousseau was a folk artist, of the same breed as Edward Hicks (compare figure 99); but strangely enough, he was also a genius. How else could he have painted a picture like *The Sleeping Gypsy* (figure 118)? You will find it difficult to escape the magic spell of this dream in paint. What goes on in this calm desert landscape under the light of the full moon needs no explanation, because none is possible, but perhaps for this very reason the scene becomes unbelievably real to us. Here at last we find that innocence and strength of feeling that Gauguin had thought so necessary for the Modern Age. That is why Rousseau, more than anyone else, may be called the godfather of twentieth-century painting.

141

PAINTING IN OUR OWN TIME

IN OUR ACCOUNT of painting since the industrial revolution, we have mentioned quite a number of "isms": Realism, Impressionism (and Post-Impressionism), Pointillism, Expressionism, Symbolism. In the twentieth century we find even more; the past fifty years have seen so many of them come and go that nobody has yet made an exact count. Now, we are apt to find "isms" of any sort confusing, or even frightening. That is why many of us will give up trying to understand modern art before we have really made a start; we don't want to cram our heads full of "isms." Actually, however, this is not necessary at all. We must always keep in mind that an "ism" is just a label to help us put things in their proper places. If it does not do that, we might as well forget about it. A good many "isms" in modern art belong to the latter kind: some of the styles or movements they are meant to label cannot be seen very clearly, while others amount to so little that only the specialist has to bother with them. After all, it is easier to think up a new label than to create something new in art that deserves a name of its own.

Still, we can't do without "isms" altogether, and for good reasons. Let us think back to the Renaissance for a moment: there we came to know many local "schools." Every country, every region, every important city had its own way of doing things, so that we often can tell at a glance where a picture of this period came from. In the Baroque era, we still found such differences, but we also saw more and more international give-and-take. Since then, this trend has grown apace. The Age of Machines has made life pretty much the same throughout the Western world; it has also forced the same problems on all of us. Today we are so involved in each other, whether we want it or not, that no man, no nation can remain an island any more. You can see then why local or national "schools" are of little importance in modern art. Their place has been taken by movements, or "isms," that have a way of spreading across all boundaries. Within this bewildering variety, however, we find three main currents, and it is these that we shall keep our eye on. They all had their start among the Post-Impressionists, but in our own century they have been carried a great deal further. One of them, Expressionism, stresses the artist's feelings about himself and the world. Another, under the name of Abstraction, is concerned with the order of shapes inside the picture. And the third, which we shall call Fantastic Art, explores the realm of imagination. At this point it is well

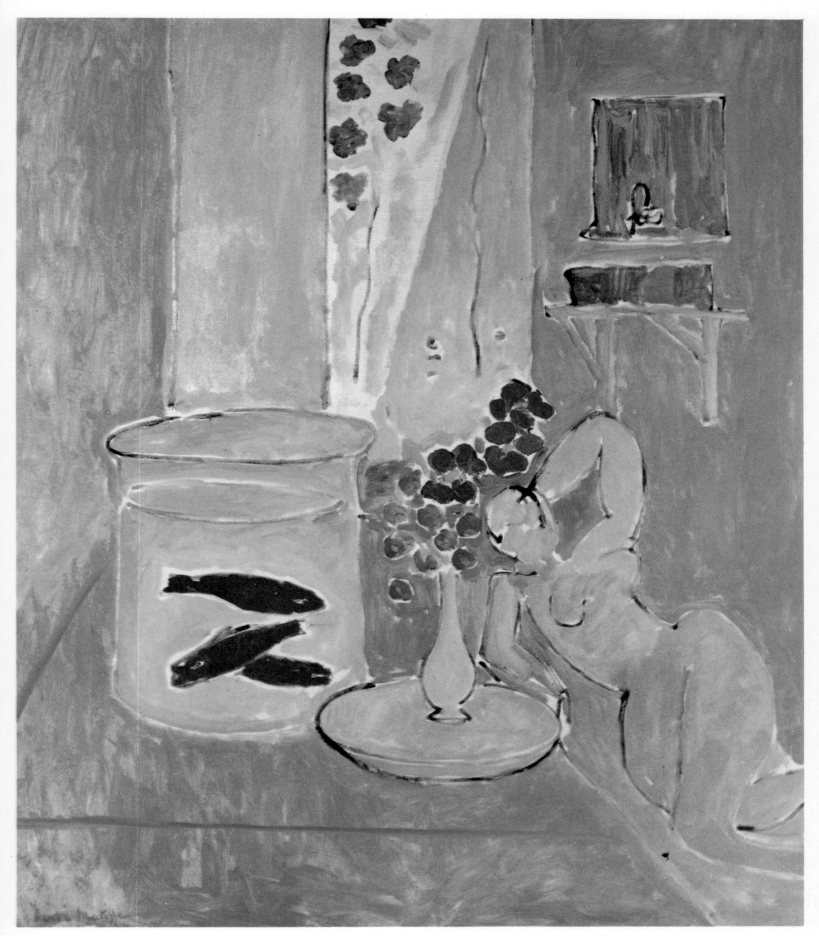

119. Matisse. STILL LIFE: GOLDFISH AND SCULPTURE. 1911. Museum of Modern Art, New York

to remember that feeling, order, and imagination go into *every* work of art: without imagination, it would be deadly dull; if it had no order at all, we should find it horribly incoherent; and if there were no feeling behind it, it would leave us completely unmoved. But of course an artist may be more interested in one of these than in the others, and that is all we mean when we speak of the three currents.

Expressionism is no longer new to us. We have seen it in van Gogh, in Gauguin, and even in Toulouse-Lautrec. These three were the artists most admired by a young Spanish painter who arrived in Paris in the year 1900. His name was Pablo Picasso. Later on, he became the most famous, as well as the most fought-over, of all living artists; but during the first few years of his career he was unknown, poor, and lonely. His state of mind is clearly reflected in *The Old Guitarist* (figure 120) of 1903, which shows one of the first of Picasso's many phases. The painting is done almost entirely in blues, the color of gloom; this underlines the hopeless feeling and makes the starved musician look even more pathetic. Picasso must have felt like an outcast himself; that is why his heart went out to those suffering in silence as this beggar does. Yet the picture is not all despair. The way the old man accepts his fate reminds us of a saint. And if we turn back to figure 66, we will find similar faces and hands among the Apostles of El Greco's *Assumption*. Our guitarist, then, is of a strange breed—part Mannerist, part Gauguin and Toulouse-Lautrec (notice the smoothly curved outlines!), filtered through the personal gloom of a twenty-two-year-old genius.

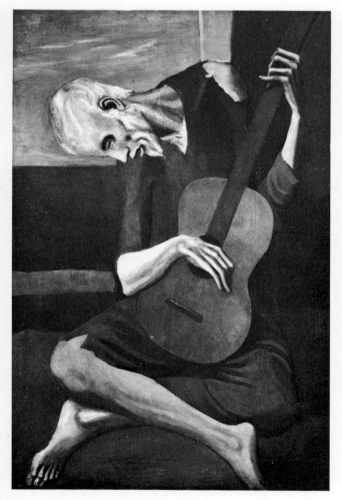

About this time, a group of young French painters were also turning to Expressionism. These men so outraged the public that they came to be known as the Fauves—that is, Wild Beasts—and they did not resent the name a bit. Their leader was Henri Matisse, another of the "old masters" of modern art (he died in 1954). His still life, *Goldfish and Sculpture* (figure 119), is less violent than the first pictures of the Fauves; it can still show us, however, why their works and ideas caused such an uproar. In its extreme simplicity, the picture certainly takes a long step beyond van Gogh and Gauguin, but not in the same direction. Here the quick "handwriting" of the brush betrays no personal anguish; it tells us, rather, that Matisse had strong feelings about one thing only—the act of painting itself. That is why his picture is such a delightful "teaser" for the eye: the bowl,

120. Picasso. OLD GUITARIST. 1903. Art Institute of Chicago

121. Modigliani. GIRL WITH BRAIDS. 1917. Collection Dr. and Mrs. Ernest Kahn, Cambridge, Mass.

the vase, and the figure are foreshortened, and the lively fish in the clear green water are startlingly "real"; the room, on the other hand, has been flattened out into one solid blue area, the yellow curtain and the view out the window are equally flat, and there is no hint of shading anywhere. It is as if Matisse had said to himself: "Let me see what I have to do to nature in order to change it into a decorative pattern, and yet keep it intact as much as I can." Nobody has ever managed this union of opposites as gracefully as he.

The excitement generated over the Fauves helped to bring a lot of modern-minded foreign artists to Paris. Among them was Amedeo Modigliani, the talented Italian painter who did the *Girl with Braids* (figure 121). He died when he was quite young, and his life was exceptionally tragic. Perhaps that explains the wistful poetic charm of this picture, which creates a mood not unlike that of Picasso's *Old Guitarist*. The style, however, with its simplified, dark outlines, its blocks of bright color, seems much closer to Matisse, although Modigliani uses

subtle bits of shading here and there to lift the head away from its background.

The work of the Fauves had a particularly strong echo in Germany, where it touched off a similar movement. *The Dream* (figure 122) is a picture by Max Beckmann, the most powerful and original of these German Expressionists. Beckmann had come to Expressionism as a result of his experiences in the First World War, which left him with a deep feeling of despair at the state of our civilization. Like Gauguin, he was an artist with a great deal to say. His problem was how to say it. In order to show what he saw behind the surface of modern life, he could not simply paint the surface itself; he needed symbols, but where was he to find them? All the old ones had long since lost their meaning—so he did what Gauguin had done: he invented his own. But because these are *new* symbols, we must not try to "read" them one by one, the way we do those of earlier times. Perhaps Beckmann himself did not know what they stand for, any more than we can explain the things we see in our own dreams. "These are the creatures that haunt my imagination," he seems to say. "To me they have the power of symbols that sum up our nightmarish present-

122. Beckmann. THE DREAM. 1921. Private Collection

123. Rouault. SEATED CLOWN. About 1939. Collection Mr. and Mrs. Alex L. Hillman, New York

124. Marin. LOWER MANHATTAN. 1920. Museum of Modern Art, New York

day world. They show you the true nature of man—how weak we are, how helpless against ourselves, in this proud era of so-called progress." His message may well remind you of Jerome Bosch (figure 34), and there is indeed something Late Gothic about Beckmann's tilted, zigzag world and its jerky, puppet-like figures. He has painted a modern "ship of fools," as forceful and disquieting as the first.

Only one other painter shows such deep concern with the state of the world: the French painter Georges Rouault, who had once exhibited with the Fauves. Rouault, however, had found assurance in his strong Christian faith, and his pictures, such as the *Seated Clown* (figure 123), suggest sympathy and pity rather than despair. His subjects, too, are less violent and of a more familiar kind. The tragic clown, outwardly gay, inwardly sad, is known to most of us,

148

but in Rouault's hands he becomes a symbol for the sufferings of all mankind. We are made to feel this from the way the picture is painted—in a style that owes much to van Gogh and Gauguin but perhaps even more to Gothic stained glass windows. Yet the expressive power of the shapes and colors belongs to Rouault alone.

Lower Manhattan (figure 124), by the American painter John Marin, shows you power of a different sort. If Rouault's picture seems to glow from within, this one fairly explodes with action. What other style could possibly give us as much of the "feel" of the big city with its crowds, its noisy traffic, its restless energy? How relaxed and leisurely the *Pont Neuf* of Renoir is in comparison, even though it was done only half a century earlier. You will hardly find a more striking illustration of the pace of modern life than the contrast between these two pictures, each of them so exactly right for the character of its subject.

But we must catch up with the second of our three currents, the one we labeled Abstraction. What does the word mean? "To abstract (from something)" means "to draw away from, to separate." If we have ten apples and then separate the ten from the apples, we have an "abstract number," since it no longer means ten particular objects. Now let us suppose we want to make a picture of our ten apples: we will find no two of them alike. If we leave out any of these small differences, we are already "abstracting" a part of what we actually see. As a matter of fact, even the most realistic portrait of our ten apples will

125. Picasso. NUDE. Drawing. 1910. Collection Alfred Stieglitz Estate

149

126. Picasso. STILL LIFE WITH CHAIR CANING. 1911–12. Collection of the Artist

127. Picasso. MOTHER AND CHILD. 1922.
Collection Mr. and Mrs. Alex L. Hillman, New York

turn out to be an "abstraction" of sorts, because we cannot do it without leaving out *something*. Abstraction, then, goes into the making of any work of art, whether the artist knows it or not. The ancient Egyptians, for instance, who drew the little "stick men" in figure 5, certainly did not realize they were abstracting, neither did the Greeks who made the Geometric vase in figure 8. In the Renaissance, however, artists began to abstract in a conscious and controlled way. They found that the shapes of nature were easier for the eye to grasp if you looked at them in terms of the simple and regular shapes of geometry (Piero della Francesca did this in figures 37 and 38). Cézanne and Seurat rediscovered this method and explored it further (compare figures 109, 110, 111); according to Cézanne, "every shape in nature is based on the sphere, the cone, and the cylinder." It was the work of these two men that really started the abstract movement in modern art.

Towards 1906, Picasso turned away from his earlier style and started painting in the manner of Cézanne. He was joined in this by his friend Georges Braque, who had been one of the Fauves until then. In the next few years, these two went a long way beyond Cézanne and created an exciting new style called Cubism. We shall understand the reason for the name if we look at Picasso's *Nude* of 1910 (figure 125), full of straight lines and right angles. But where is the nude figure? It is not easy to find at first, so we have tried to disentangle it in a sketch of our own, a sort of "skeleton key" to the picture (which may be found on page 163). At this point, however, we might be even more puzzled than before. Why did the artist insist on hiding a nude among all these shapes? Would not the angles and planes have made a more beautiful design if they did not have to represent anything at all? There were some

150

128. Braque. LE COURRIER. Collage. 1913. Philadelphia Museum of Art

129. Picasso. THREE MUSICIANS. 1921. Philadelphia Museum of Art, A. E. Gallatin Collection

later artists who believed that, but not Picasso. To him, as to Cézanne, abstraction was "what you did to nature in order to make if fit the picture"; it had no meaning by itself. He uses much tighter rules of order here than Cézanne ever did—rules that almost force him to break the human form apart entirely—but he still needs nature to challenge his creative powers. In other words, what counts is neither the nude nor the design, but the tension between the two.

In figure 126, Picasso has applied the same rules to a still life. Everything is broken up into angles and planes except the three letters (whose shapes cannot be made more abstract than they are to begin with). But how can we explain the piece of imitation chair caning pasted into the picture? Why the oval shape, and the rope instead of a frame? Picasso apparently wanted to make the canvas look like a tray on which the still life is "served" to us. It is a rather witty notion of his to put the abstract "shapes of things" on top of the real things (canvas, chair caning, and rope). Picasso probably did not realize it right then and there, but he had just started to invent a new language of painting. The still life *Le Courrier* by Braque (figure 128), done a year later, shows you the next step in the growth of this new language. Here the main parts of the design are pasted together out of odd pieces of paper (this is called collage, the French word for "pasting"), with only a few drawn lines and bits of shading added to make it complete. As a result, the real and the abstract have become so thoroughly mixed up that we can no longer ask: "What is this a picture of?" Even more than before, the white paper acts as a "tray," but does the tray hold the *picture* of a still life, or the still life itself? The meaning, then, is a good deal more complicated here than in Picasso's *Nude*, but the means have become very much simpler, since they can be found in any wastebasket.

Actually, it must have been a great strain on the artist to create balance and harmony from these chance pickings; a fine collage, such as the Braque, is a rare and beautiful thing. That is why Braque and Picasso did not continue this technique for very long. Soon they took the final step towards the new language: they began to do pictures that looked like collage but were actually painted with the brush. We can see the results in Picasso's *Three Musicians* (figure 129), one of the great masterpieces of modern times. This picture has both the size and the monumental feeling of a mural; its precisely "cut" shapes are fitted together as firmly as building blocks, yet they are not ends

130. Demuth. MY EGYPT. 1925. Whitney Museum, New York

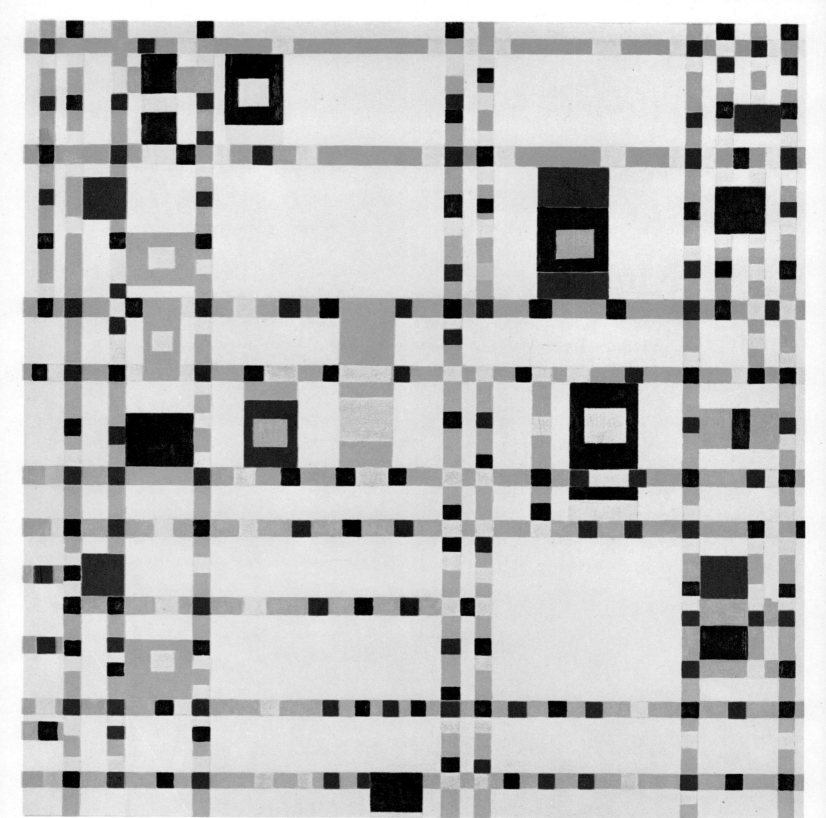

131. Mondrian. BROADWAY BOOGIE-WOOGIE. 1941–42. Museum of Modern Art, New York

in themselves (if they were, the painting would look like a patchwork quilt). Every one of them has a definite meaning, and the image of the three seated, masked figures, translated into this new language, emerges more and more strongly the longer we look at it. There is space here, too, although not the kind we know from the "window-pictures" of the Renaissance; instead of looking *through* the canvas into depth, we see space in terms of the overlapping layers of shapes *in front* of the canvas. That is why Picasso can now do without shading entirely, while

153

in the two earlier stages of Cubism he still needed it. At this point let us turn back to another musician, done some fifty years earlier: Manet's *Fife Player* (figure 103). Does he not strike us as the true grandfather of our Picasso? He should, for it was shadowless paintings such as this one that started off the "revolution of the color patch" which had its final triumph in Collage-Cubism.

For Picasso, however, there could be no standing still. Once Collage-Cubism was fully worked out, he had begun to show greater interest in representation, and by the time he did the *Three Musicians* he also painted Neo-Classic pictures such as the *Mother and Child* of figure 127. Here the bodies are as rounded and heavy as carved stone; it is this monumental quality, in fact, that links the two pictures together, different though they seem in so many other ways. Picasso has now returned to the warm, human world of his early works, but with a new strength of form that he owes to his Cubist experience.

Meanwhile, the influence of Cubism had spread far and wide, not only in painting but in sculpture, in the decorative arts, and even into architecture. Many painters felt that Cubism, as an abstract "system" of shapes, had a great deal in common with science and engineering and that, for this reason, it was the only style for putting the industrial landscape of the Age of Machines on canvas. We can judge for ourselves how true this is from our next two pictures. In *My Egypt* (figure 130), the American painter Charles Demuth has done to some factory buildings what Picasso did to his *Nude*; but since his "model" was made by man, rather than by nature (and was thus closer to abstraction from the very start) he did not have to change it so much. Demuth saw his main task in bringing out the hidden force and impressiveness of

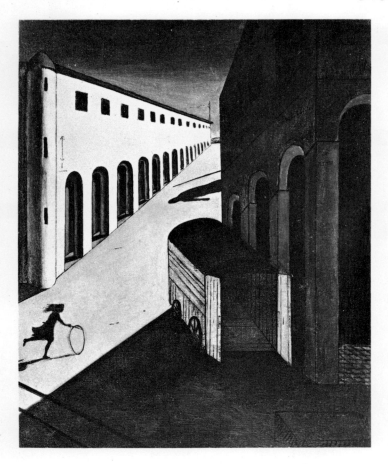

these industrial shapes. In his canvas, they loom so large that they almost frighten us. However, he also asks a question: "These are the pyramids of modern times; they are our claim to greatness. Will they last as long as the monuments of old?"

Broadway Boogie-Woogie (figure 131), done by the Dutch painter Piet Mondrian between 1941 and 1942, shortly before his death in this country, is a more exciting picture in many ways. Mondrian was the strictest and most "architectural" of all abstract painters. He limited his palette to the primary colors, and his pictures are made up entirely of solid squares or rectangles, while all the lines have to go either straight up-and-down or across. Now

132. De Chirico. MELANCHOLY AND MYSTERY OF A STREET. 1914. Collection Mr. and Mrs. Stanley Resor, New York

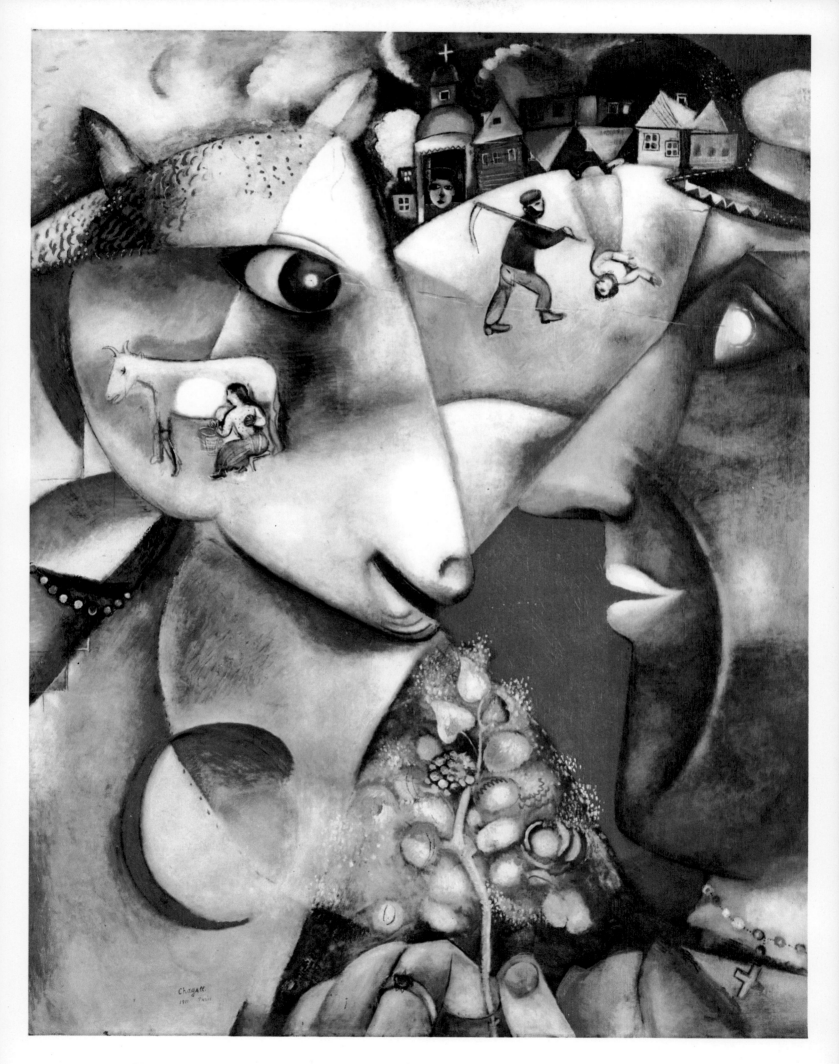

133. Chagall. I AND THE VILLAGE. 1911. Museum of Modern Art, New York (Mrs. Simon Guggenheim Fund)

one might think that a language with such a small "vocabulary" cannot possibly say a great deal, but Mondrian's painting proves that this need not be true at all; in fact, it has a spine-tingling liveliness unmatched by any other picture in this book. The entire design moves with the pulse beat of the big city—its flashing neon signs, its stop-and-go traffic along precisely laid-out patterns. As a picture of the kind of life modern man has created for himself out of his mastery over the forces of nature, *Broadway Boogie-Woogie* makes Marin's *Lower Manhattan*, done only twenty years earlier, look curiously out-of-date.

Our third current, the one we termed "Fantasy," follows a less clear-cut course than the other two, since it depends more on a state of mind than on any particular style. The only thing all painters of fantasy have in common is the belief that "seeing with the inner eye" is more important than looking at the world outside; and since every artist has his own private inner world, his way of telling us about it is apt to be just as personal. But why should any body *want* to tell us about his private world of daydreams and nightmares? And how could it possibly mean anything to us, since our own is bound to be different from his? It seems, though, that we are not as different from each other as all that. Our minds are all built on the same pattern, even if we don't all have equally good ones. And that goes for imagination and memory, too. These belong to the unconscious part of our mind, which we cannot control at will. That is where all our experiences are stored up, whether we want to remember them or not; and at night, or whenever we are not thinking of anything in particular, they come back to us, and we seem to live through them again. However, the unconscious part of our minds usually

does not give us back our experiences the way they actually happened. It likes to disguise them as "dream images" so that they become less vivid and real to us and we can live with our memories more easily. This digesting of experiences is just as important as the proper digesting of food for our inner well-being.

Now, the way our unconscious mind digests our experiences is pretty much alike in all of us, although it works better with some people than with others. That is why we are always interested in learning about imaginary things, if the person who tells us about them knows how to make them seem real. What happens in a fairy tale, for example, makes no logical sense at all in the matter-of-fact language of a news report, but

134. Klee. CONQUEST OF THE MOUNTAIN. 1939.
Collection Aline Saarinen, New York

135. Klee. TWITTERING MACHINE. 1922. Museum of Modern Art, New York

when somebody tells it "correctly" our imaginations are stimulated. The same holds true for painting. We have already seen one very beautiful and impressive "fairy-tale picture," Rousseau's *Sleeping Gypsy* (figure 118); perhaps we shall like some of the later ones just as well.

Melancholy and Mystery of a Street (figure 132), by the Italian painter Giorgio de Chirico, comes closest to the imaginary reality of the *Sleeping Gypsy*. We cannot explain any of the strange things that happen in it, yet the eerie feeling of the whole is so familiar to us that we know right away it must be a dream we are looking at. But de Chirico, who was no folk artist, had a mind much more complicated than Rousseau's. That is why his dream world seems so troubled with hidden fears, as against the wonderful calmness of the earlier picture. Marc Chagall's *I and the Village* (figure 133), in contrast, enchants us by its gaiety. In this "Cubist fairy tale," dreamlike memories of Russian folk stories and of the Russian countryside have been woven together into a glowing vision. Chagall here relives the experiences of his childhood, experiences so important to him that his imagination shaped and re-shaped them for years without ever getting rid of their memories.

The "fairy tales" of the Swiss painter Paul Klee are far more purposeful and controlled than those of Chagall, even though at first they may strike us as more childlike. Klee, too, had been influenced by Cubism, but he refined and pared it down into a marvelously precise language of his own. His aim was always to create "signs," which means shapes that are images of ideas the way the *shape* "A" is an image of the *sound* "A"; except, of course, that Klee's ideas are

very much more intricate than that. One of the simpler ones is his *Twittering Machine* (figure 135), where he mocks the Age of Machines by inventing a sort of mechanical ghost that imitates bird noises. *The Conquest of the Mountain* (figure 134), on the other hand, shows a real machine—a locomotive—behaving in human fashion. As it puffs up the mountainside, it glows with effort, just like a climber who gets red in the face from doing the same thing. In this picture, done shortly before his death, Klee's imagination is as fresh, his sense of wonder as strong as ever; at the same time, every shape has a rightness and dignity about it that betray the most serious artistic effort.

The Spaniard Joan Miró will remind you of Klee in some ways. His *Harlequin's Carnival* (figure 137) looks like something one might

136. Ernst. COLLAGE. 1920.
Hagenbach Collection, France

158

137. Miró. THE HARLEQUIN'S CARNIVAL. 1924–25. Albright-Knox Art Gallery, Buffalo, New York

see under a fairy-tale microscope—a lively and colorful miniature stage where everybody and everything is full of magic tricks. However, Miró also had been a Cubist before he discovered his own world of fantasy, and the effortless gaiety of our picture is actually the result of painstaking care in the design of every detail.

Figure 136 shows us a different kind of fantasy, haunted and disturbing like the dreams of de Chirico. This is a collage by Max Ernst, one of the leaders of the Dada movement at the end of the First World War. The Dadaists were so revolted by the cruelty of the war that they declared Western civilization bankrupt from beginning to end. They felt they must start from scratch, respecting only one law, the law of chance, and only one reality, that of their own imaginations. Their main task, they thought, was to shock the public into the same unsettled frame of mind, and they tried to do this by exhibiting their creations, most of which were spur-of-the-moment "gestures" meant to defy all reason. Our collage is more serious than that—in fact, desperately so. It is made up of cuttings from pictures of machinery and other technical equipment, which have been pasted together so as to form two nightmarish "mechanical men." These stare at us blindly through their goggles and demand to know if we recognize them as

159

images of modern man, slave to the machine and thus little more than a machine himself.

Yet the Dada movement was not all negative. It actually helped painters to rediscover and make use of chance effects for artistic creation, as a counterweight to the purposeful discipline of Cubism. Those who believed in "taking a chance" and letting their imaginations flow unchecked, founded the Surrealist movement, with Max Ernst as one of its leading spirits. It was he who introduced (or revived, rather) the technique so skillfully employed in the drawing by Salvador Dali (figure 138). If you look carefully, you will see that the main shapes in the *Landscape with Figures* (the rocks, the beach, and the clouds) are actually ink blots made by chance, just like the one illustrated at the beginning this book. All Dali had to do was to see a picture "into" the blots and then fill in the missing lines, so that others can see it, too. This does not mean that the drawing is less of a work of art because Dali has accepted the "help" of the ink blots. It does show us again, though, that the way our imagination works is still the same as in the days of the cavemen who saw animals in the bumps on the cave walls. Only the things we imagine, and the way we put them into pictures, have changed. These changes are what the history of painting is about.

138. Dali. LANDSCAPE WITH FIGURES. 1936. Collection Schaeffer Galleries, New York

INDEX

All references are to page numbers. Light-face numerals indicate text references; **bold-face numerals** refer to black-and-white illustrations; and **bold-face numerals (within parentheses),** to the colorplates. Titles of all illustrations are in italics.

139. Skeleton Key to Figure 125

Van Goyen, Jan, **91,** 94, 96
Van Ruisdael, Jacob, **92,** 96
Van der Weyden, Roger, **(41),** 44–46
Vase paintings, 16–19
Velázquez, Diego, **98, (99),** 100
Venus, The Birth of, by Botticelli, 56, **(57)**
Vermeer, Jan, **(97),** 98
Veronese, **(69),** 71

Victorious David, The, by Castagno, **(51),** 54
Village Bride, The, by Greuze, **104,** 105–106

Watson and the Shark, by Copley, **108,** 110
Watteau, Antoine, 102, **(103),** 104
Wax painting, method of, 19
West, Benjamin, **(109),** 110

Wild Beasts, *see* Fauves
Woodcut, **72,** 74, **136,** 140

Yellow Christ, The, by Gauguin, **(137),** 138–140
Yonkers Ramp and His Sweetheart, by Hals, **(87),** 92
Youth, by Bouguereau, **127,** 128

Zacharias and the Angel, **(27),** 30

ACKNOWLEDGMENTS

THE AUTHORS AND PUBLISHER wish to acknowledge the courtesy of the following museums and private collectors in permitting the reproduction of paintings or drawings:

AMSTERDAM, Rijksmuseum (figure 79). ANTWERP, Museum (figure 69). ATHENS, National Museum (figure 10). BERLIN, State Museums (figures 42, 61). BOSTON, Museum of Fine Arts (figures 76, 87, 90); Isavella Stewart Gardner Museum (figure 74). BRUSSELS, Musée Royal (figure 92). BUFFALO, Albright-Knox Art Gallery (figure 115). CAMBRIDGE, MASS., Fogg Museum of Art (figure 112). CHANTILLY, Musée Condé (figure 25). CHICAGO, Art Institute (figures 66, 95, 111, 117, 120). COLMAR, Musée Unterlinden (figure 56). DIJON, Museum (figure 26). DRESDEN, Gemäldegalerie (figures 54, 77, 102). DUBLIN, Trinity College Library (figure 17). FLORENCE, Uffizi Gallery (figures 27, 39, 44). THE HAGUE, Mauritshuis (figure 75). INDIANAPOLIS, John Herron Art Institute (figure 109). LONDON, National Gallery (figures 30, 97); Tate Gallery (figure 89). LYONS, Museum (figure 108). Madrid, Prado Museum (figures 81, 82, 94). MANCHESTER, Art Gallery (figure 98). MUNICH, Pinakothek (figures 58, 70). NEW YORK, The Frick Collection (figures 53, 73); Metropolitan Museum (8, 9, 11, 12, 13, 21, 29, 31, 34, 72, 83, 85, 100, 104, 107); Museum of Modern Art (figures 118, 119, 124, 131, 133, 135, 137); Pierpont Morgan Library (figure 19); Whitney Museum of American Art (figure 130). OSLO, National Gallery (figure 116). OTTERLO, Kröller-Müller State Museum (figure 113). PARIS, Bibliothèque Nationale (figure 22); Louvre Museum (frontispiece, figures 24, 32, 34, 41, 46, 50, 51, 52, 62, 84, 86, 93, 96, 103). PHILADELPHIA, Museum of Art (figures 127, 129). ROTTERDAM, Boymans Museum (figure 78). STOCKHOLM, National Museum (figure 71). VENICE, Accademia (figure 55). VIENNA, Kunsthistorische Sammlungen (figures 18, 57, 63, 80). WASHINGTON, D. C., National Gallery of Art (fignres 16, 36, 40, 91, 101). WINDSOR CASTLE (figure 45). WORCESTER, Art Museum (figures 43, 99).

Mr. G. W. Andrews, Redhill, Surrey (figure 88); M. Jean Arp, Meudon (figure 136); Mrs. Robert Boggs, New York (figure 105); Mr. and Mrs. Alex L. Hillman, New York (figures 123, 127); Dr. and Mrs. Ernest Kahn, Cambridge, Mass. (figure 121); M. René Lecomte, Paris (figure 110); Mr. Robert Lehman, New York (figure 33); Mrs. Aline Saarinen, New York (figure 134); Miss Georgia O'Keefe, New York (figure 125, from the Estate of Alfred Stieglitz); Mr. and Mrs. Stanley Resor, New York (figure 132).

Photographs have been supplied by the owners of the works of art reproduced, except for the following: A.C.L., Brussels (figure 69); Alinari, Florence (figures 10, 27); Anderson, Rome (figures 47, 49); Braun & Cie, Mulhouse (figures 52, 67, 84, 106); Bruckmann A. G., Munich (figures 54, 63, 75, 77); A. C. Cooper, Ltd., London (figures 88, 98); Pierre Devinoy, Paris (figure 20); Foto Marburg (figure 22); Mas, Barcelona (figure 81); Pontificia Commissione per Archaeologia Sacra, Rome (figure 14); Soprintendenza alle gallerie, Florence (figures 35, 65).

In addition, the courtesy of the following institutions and individuals in supplying photographs is gratefully acknowledged: Museum of Fine Arts, Boston (figure 60); Metropolitan Museum of Art, New York (figure 6); Museum of Modern Art, New York (figures 114, 125, 126, 130, 132, 136); Netherlands Institute for Art History, The Hague (figure 78); The Warburg Institute, London (figure 39); Mr. William Chapman, New York (figure 4, from the color film, "Lascaux: Cradle of Man's Art"); Mr. Hans S. Schaeffer, New York (figure 138); Mr. Curt Valentin, New York (figures 122, 128).